AFRICAN ETHNOGRAPHIC STUDIES OF THE 20TH CENTURY

Volume 25

EFIK TRADERS OF OLD CALABAR

EFIK TRADERS OF OLD CALABAR

Containing
the Diary of Antera Duke
together with
an Ethnographic Sketch and Notes
and an Essay on
the Political Organization of Old Calabar

Edited by
DARYLL FORDE

LONDON AND NEW YORK

First published in 1956 by Oxford University Press for the International African
Institute.

This edition first published in 2018
by Routledge
2 Park Square, Milton Park, Abingdon, Oxon OX14 4RN

and by Routledge
711 Third Avenue, New York, NY 10017

Routledge is an imprint of the Taylor & Francis Group, an informa business

© 1956 International African Institute

All rights reserved. No part of this book may be reprinted or reproduced or utilised
in any form or by any electronic, mechanical, or other means, now known or
hereafter invented, including photocopying and recording, or in any information
storage or retrieval system, without permission in writing from the publishers.

Trademark notice: Product or corporate names may be trademarks or registered
trademarks, and are used only for identification and explanation without intent to
infringe.

British Library Cataloguing in Publication Data
A catalogue record for this book is available from the British Library

ISBN: 978-0-8153-8713-8 (Set)
ISBN: 978-0-429-48813-9 (Set) (ebk)
ISBN: 978-1-138-58638-3 (Volume 25) (hbk)
ISBN: 978-0-429-50428-0 (Volume 25) (ebk)

Publisher's Note
The publisher has gone to great lengths to ensure the quality of this reprint but
points out that some imperfections in the original copies may be apparent.

Disclaimer
The publisher has made every effort to trace copyright holders and would welcome
correspondence from those they have been unable to trace.

EFIK TRADERS OF OLD CALABAR

Edited by DARYLL FORDE

Containing
THE DIARY OF ANTERA DUKE
an Efik Slave-Trading Chief of
the eighteenth century

together with
AN ETHNOGRAPHIC SKETCH
AND NOTES
by D. SIMMONS

and an Essay on
THE POLITICAL ORGANIZATION OF
OLD CALABAR
by G. I. JONES

Published for the
INTERNATIONAL AFRICAN INSTITUTE
by the
OXFORD UNIVERSITY PRESS
LONDON   NEW YORK   TORONTO
1956

Oxford University Press, Amen House, London E.C.4
GLASGOW NEW YORK TORONTO MELBOURNE WELLINGTON
BOMBAY CALCUTTA MADRAS KARACHI CAPE TOWN IBADAN

PRINTED IN GREAT BRITAIN

CONTENTS

	Page
Map of Old Calabar at the Cross River Estuary	vi
Introduction *by Daryll Forde*	vii
An Ethnographic Sketch of the Efik people *by D. Simmons*	1
The Diary of Antera Duke, being three years in the life of an Efik chief, 18th January 1785 to 31st January 1788, in a modern English version *by A. W. Wilkie and D. Simmons*	27
Notes on the Diary *by D. Simmons*	66
The Original Text of the Diary *by Antera Duke*	79
The Political Organization of Old Calabar *by G. I. Jones*	116
Addendum *by G. I. Jones*	158
Bibliography	161
Index	163

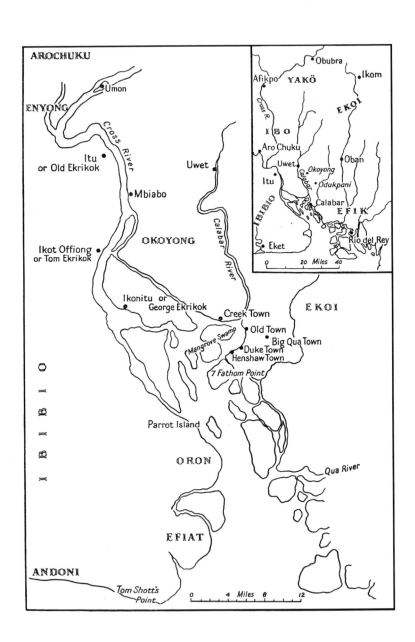

INTRODUCTION

THE Efik of Old Calabar, on the Cross River estuary in what is now the Calabar Province of Nigeria, were famous in the eighteenth and nineteenth centuries among the trading peoples of the Oil Rivers of West Africa. This stretch of the West African coast, which included the Niger Delta and the estuary of the Cross and Calabar rivers, took its name from the trade in palm-oil which developed in place of the notorious slave-trade that was gradually suppressed by the British in the first half of the nineteenth century. The main rivers and the innumerable creeks here provided a network of waterways into the interior, which the slave-raiders and oil traders commanded with their fleets of large canoes. From their coastal settlements these African traders dealt with their European counterparts who lived in their ships that were moored close by. In return for slaves and oil they obtained supplies of European goods, and not least the firearms which enabled them to dominate the hinterland. The wealth and power to which this gave rise led to the growth of considerable communities and of miniature but fiercely competitive trading empires in such centres as Bonny, Brass and later Opobo, on the Niger Delta, and in Old Calabar.

The Efik, originally a small branch of the Ibibio-speaking peoples who had moved south-east to waterside settlements on the Cross River estuary where they lived mainly as fishermen, had found their opportunity in the slave-trade. Their communities grew and multiplied during the seventeenth and eighteenth centuries with the success of this traffic. Some outstanding features of their life have long been known from the vivid accounts of events and customs written by early European travellers and traders and later by the British Consuls and the missionaries. These have described the wealth, prestige and pomp of the 'houses' of successful

viii EFIK TRADERS OF OLD CALABAR

trader-chiefs and the remarkable power of the Egbo Society—
a graded association of freemen which controlled and was
controlled by the wealthy leaders of the Efik towns.

In their relations with the European traders, who were for
the most part fleeting visitors with neither the interest nor the
training to learn an African language, the Efik soon appreci-
ated the importance of acquiring a trade language in which to
carry out their transactions. Thus at Old Calabar, and in the
other trading centres of the Oil Rivers, there developed,
through intercourse with the English traders and seamen, a
jargon which was mainly English in vocabulary although the
constructions were often modelled on those of Ibibio. Europeans adopted it in their dealings with Africans and it was
carried from place to place on the West Coast where it
merged with other jargons, similarly developed, to become
in the eighteenth century a fairly standardized pidgin
English.

The value of written records, especially of transactions, was
also recognized by the Efik traders, and some of them were
effectively instructed in writing by Englishmen from the
ships. Several published narratives of the early nineteenth
century refer to the keeping of accounts and journals by the
leading Efik at this time. Adams[1] recorded that already in the
eighteenth century the sons of some of the traders had visited
England and that schools had been established by the Efik
in their towns 'for the purpose of instructing in this art the
youth belonging to families of consequence'. Robertson[2]
quoted passages from a manuscript written by a leading chief,
Eyo Honesty, at the beginning of the nineteenth century.
It was, moreover, at the request of Efik notables, largely on
account of their desire for schooling, that the Church of
Scotland Mission arrived at Calabar in the forties of last
century.

Unfortunately, few, if any, of these early Efik documents

[1] J. Adams, *Sketches taken during Ten Voyages to Africa between the Years
1786 and 1800*, London, 1823, p. 40.

[2] G. A. Robertson, *Notes on Africa*, London, 1819, pp. 313-18.

INTRODUCTION

appear to have survived or to have been closely studied. It was, therefore, with great interest that we learnt of the preservation of part of a diary written at Calabar in the late eighteenth century by Antera Duke, a leading trader and senior member of Egbo. This has afforded an opportunity, not merely to publish an important document concerning the history of Old Calabar, but also to provide an ethnographic background and a sociological interpretation for this and other early writings on the Efik.

Antera Duke's diary was brought to the notice of the Institute by the Rev. Dr. A. W. Wilkie, C.B.E., formerly of the Church of Scotland Mission, Calabar. The original text, consisting of daily entries for the years 1785 to 1788, was written in Antera Duke's own hand in a large folio volume—such as might have been used as a ship's log-book—which had, apparently, been given to him by one of the officers of a slave-ship anchored off Duke Town, Calabar. The volume was brought to Scotland some time during the nineteenth century by a missionary from Calabar and deposited in the library of the United Presbyterian Church offices in Edinburgh. After the union of this Church with the Free Church of Scotland, the library was transferred to new offices in George Street, Edinburgh, and placed under the care of the late Mr. William Valentine, at that time a senior clerk in the Foreign Mission Offices of the Church and later Assistant Foreign Mission Secretary. Mr. Valentine discovered the diary and showed it to Dr. Wilkie who immediately recognized its great historical interest. Having read the whole diary with care—and some difficulty, for discoloration of the paper and fading of the ink made portions of it hard to decipher— Dr. Wilkie made a number of lengthy extracts from it before returning the volume. During the war the offices of the United Church of Scotland suffered bombing and, though measures had been taken to store books and records in safety, some of these—including, it is feared, Antera Duke's diary— were unfortunately destroyed. The extracts made and preserved by Dr. Wilkie, are, therefore, all that remains of a fascinating personal record, which is also a unique and valuable source of information on the social life and customs of the Efik people and their relations with European traders nearly 200 years ago.

The diary was written in pidgin English, and Dr. Wilkie, besides copying the original text, made a 'translation' into English. The text which follows is Dr. Wilkie's version, revised, with his permission, in consultation with Mr. Simmons. The extracts from the original diary copied by Dr. Wilkie are also printed in full.

Soon after Dr. Wilkie had been good enough to send the diary to the Institute, with permission to publish it in suitable form, Mr. Donald Simmons of Yale University returned from a period of ethnographic and linguistic enquiry among the Efik. He readily agreed to provide an ethnographic introduction to the diary and to annotate it in detail to bring out the significance of Antera Duke's often cryptic entries. Mr. Eyo B. Ndem, M.A., himself an Efik, also contributed some notes, including an account of the Efik mourning ceremonies. Meanwhile, it so happened that Mr. G. I. Jones of Cambridge University, who knew the Ibibio well from his previous service among them in the Nigerian Administration, was studying the early sources and later reports on the Oil Rivers settlements and offered to contribute an essay on the character and development of Efik political organization. This essay has, accordingly, been included in the present volume. The ethnographic sketch by Mr. Simmons and Mr. Jones's essay were written independently and, for the most part, deal with different aspects of life in Old Calabar. Both authors, have, however, been good enough to agree to some editorial revision and rearrangement of their studies in order to relate them to one another and to the scheme of the volume as a whole.

The early accounts, though they gave vivid and often detailed descriptions of particular incidents or aspects of the life of these peoples, afford only partial and often baffling glimpses of the organization of Efik society and of the ways in which it reacted to the impact of contemporary political and

INTRODUCTION

economic forces. Mr. Jones has sought, from a reconsideration of these records in the light of our more considerable knowledge of Ibibio ethnography and of the social processes known to be characteristic of societies of this type, to analyse the structure and development of the Efik communities and to interpret some of their more striking features. He discusses the way in which the powerful Efik 'houses' appear to have developed from small localized lineages of the kind still found in other Ibibio communities. Under the stimulus of external commerce, and with the accession of dependants, successful lineages grew into considerable corporations, often several hundred strong, under the authority of the head of the house. Despite their polygynous marriages and numerous offspring, the lineage which formed the nucleus of such a house and within which succession to its leadership was normally vested, came to form only a small minority among the other households of free-born dependants and slaves.

Mr. Jones has also been interested in an apparent contrast, during the nineteenth century, between the turbulent upheavals in most of the other Oil Rivers settlements and the comparatively stable conditions in Old Calabar. The former, although they were more compact communities and, in the case of Bonny and New Calabar, had a predominant chiefly dynasty of considerable prestige, were frequently riven by factions and violent rebellions which resulted on occasion in the expulsion of dissident groups. Opobo, the last of the Oil Rivers ports to emerge as a trading centre, had been founded in this way by a secession from Bonny. Old Calabar consisted of several neighbouring, but separate, settlements or towns, claiming distinct origins. There was no one clearly predominant group and no paramount chieftaincy. Between them competition for slaves, oil and the European trade was great. This was a setting in which hostilities and violence might have been expected to arise. And indeed there had been prolonged fighting in the eighteenth century between the two chief rivals, Old Town and Duke Town. Raids and ambushes by each on the canoes of the other were so constant in the

xii EFIK TRADERS OF OLD CALABAR

1760's that, according to Captain Hall's account,[1] trade almost ceased until some of the Europeans intervened to assist Duke Town to attack and plunder Old Town. But from that time on, and notably during the great expansion of the palm-oil trade in the later nineteenth century, despite the commercial jealousies between the towns and between leading houses within them, an effective unity was maintained at Calabar both within and between the various settlements.

The earlier and more effective suppression of the slave-trade at Calabar, access to which was more easily controlled by the naval squadron based on Fernando Po, and the smoother transition to a rapidly expanding trade in palm-oil in which Old Calabar was the pioneer, no doubt contributed to this more peaceful development. But significance also attaches to the means by which this restraint was exercised. For in Calabar, but not in Bonny, there developed in the Egbo Society an association which, operating in all the towns, commanded, in their own interest, the allegiance of the majority of the houses and could avert or quell attempts by the powerful to build up armed factions and resort to open violence. In the Egbo Society the Efik had adopted and adapted to their own circumstances the organization and symbols of a secret society which they found in operation as an institution of village government among the Ejagham Ekoi, when they settled on the east bank of the Cross River estuary. Antera Duke's diary provides an early account by one of its leading members of the way in which Egbo intervened to enforce the settlement of disputes and impose penalties for serious breaches of custom.

The later barbarities of Old Calabar were associated, not with internecine warfare, but mainly with the obsequies of leading men when wives, retainers and other slaves were sacrificed. On these occasions, rival houses competed in the scale of their destructive display. The deaths of their leaders also led to wholesale charges of witchcraft between different houses or rival groups within them. Such accusations could

[1] Captain John Hall in *Abridgement of the Minutes of Evidence*, 1790, p. 207.

INTRODUCTION xiii

be effectively asserted and tested only by submission to the poison ordeal, which frequently proved fatal and often involved many persons on both sides.

These outbreaks of mutual destruction, Mr. Jones suggests, were symptomatic of severe tensions, both between and within the houses, which were debarred from other outlets by Egbo. On the other hand, the solidarity among the wealthy and powerful leaders of houses, which was fostered by their collective control of Egbo, produced other cleavages in Efik society, and he sees in the rise of the Blood Men, and their massing in force to prevent wholesale sacrifices, a manifestation of the opposition of the poorer freemen and slaves in the outlying villages to the excesses of an arrogant plutocracy.

DARYLL FORDE

London, 1956

NOTE ON ORTHOGRAPHY

In the Ethnographic sketch and the Notes on the Diary the following symbols are used:

ɔ—representing the vowel sound in the English word 'law';

ŋ—representing the final consonant sound in the English word 'sing'.

AN ETHNOGRAPHIC SKETCH OF
THE EFIK PEOPLE

D. Simmons[1]

THE Efik inhabit seven settlements on the lower Calabar and Cross rivers in Calabar Province, Nigeria. The two main ones, *Obio Oko*, 'Creek Town', and *Atakpa*, 'Duke Town', are situated thirty miles from the mouth of the Cross river, at latitude 4' 58" North, longitude 8' 17" East.

The name Efik is derived from the Ibibio-Efik verb root *fik*, meaning 'oppress'. Other Ibibio-speaking groups nicknamed the Efik thus because they prevented other Cross River tribes from establishing direct trade relations with European ships. The Efik refer to themselves as *Efik*, *Efik Eburutu*, and *Iboku*. Although Goldie[2] recorded in 1874 that the word *eburutu* was an eponym, no folk etymology for the word now exists. Efik claim that the name *Iboku* is derived from two Ibo words meaning 'those who quarrel with the Ibo'.

Hutchinson[3] estimated the population of Duke Town and Creek Town at 4,000 and 3,000 respectively in the middle of the nineteenth century. The 1944–5 Nominal Tax Rolls enumerate 6,400 adult males of fifteen to sixty-five years of age.[4] At the present time the Efik population probably totals 25,000 persons.

[1] The writer desires to express his gratitude to the Nigerian Government for permission to study in Calabar Province in 1952-3, to the Church of Scotland Mission and its missionaries for the many kindnesses shown to him, and to the Department of Anthropology, Yale University, for a grant which aided his research.

[2] H. Goldie, *Efik Dictionary*, 1874, p. 58.

[3] T. Hutchinson, *Impressions of Western Africa*, 1858, pp. 115, 133.

[4] D. Forde and G. I. Jones, *The Ibo and Ibibio-speaking Peoples of South-eastern Nigeria*, 1950, p. 87. The figure cited above includes the population data from Table XIX for the Efik proper, Mbiabo, Mbiabo 2, Adiabo and Efut.

EFIK TRADERS OF OLD CALABAR

Neighbouring tribes include the Ibibio, Oron, Efut, Kwa, Efiat, Okoyong, Uwet, Enyong, and Arochuku Ibo. The Ibibio and Oron live on the west side of the lower Cross River, the Efut near the mouth of the Calabar River, and the Kwa in several villages east of Duke Town, having originally migrated from the Ejagham Ekoi of the Oban Hills district. The Okoyong migrated from the Ododop group of the southern Cameroons and settled ten miles north of Creek Town. The Uwet, or Bakpinka as they call themselves, inhabit one settlement on the upper reaches of the Calabar River about thirty-five miles north of Creek Town. The Uwet claim relationship with the Umon, who live on an island in the Cross River. The Enyong inhabit several villages in the vicinity of Enyong Creek, a minor tributary of the Cross River. The Arochuku Ibo live a few miles north of the Enyong villages.

Efik is the best-known dialect of the Ibibio language group since Goldie published a grammar, Ward analysed the phonetic and tonal structure, and both Goldie and Adams compiled dictionaries.[1] Westermann and Bryan[2] establish an Ibibio-Efik group having six dialects: Ibibio, Anyang, Enyong, Eket, Andoni-Ibeno, and Efik. Greenberg[3] includes Efik in the Central Branch (Cross River Languages) of his Niger-Congo family. A comparison of 195 Ibibio and Efik words on the Swadesh basic vocabulary list revealed 189 cognates (95·89 per cent.); this very high percentage indicates that the two languages have separated only within the last few centuries.

Efik has become generally accepted as the literary language of the Ibibio dialects, following the Church of Scotland

[1] R. F. G. Adams, *Efik-English Vocabulary*, 2nd edition, 1943; H. Goldie, op. cit., and *Principles of Efik Grammar with Specimens of the Language*, 1868; I. C. Ward, *The Phonetic and Tonal Structure of Efik*, 1933.

[2] D. Westermann and M. A. Bryan, *The Languages of West Africa*, 1952.

[3] J. Greenberg, 'Studies in African Linguistic Classification, I. The Niger-Congo Family', *Southwestern Journal of Anthropology*, V. 1949, pp. 79-100.

THE EFIK PEOPLE

Mission's translation of the Bible into Efik, and owing also to the influence of Efik traders, whose peregrinations caused it to become the *lingua franca* of the lower Cross River area.[1] An extensive investigation of Efik and Ibibio vocabularies has yielded no evidence to support the contention of Jeffreys[2] that Efik is poorer in vocabulary than Ibibio, and corrupted in pronunciation through the assimilation of foreign slaves. No morphological linguistic variation occurs in the speech of Efik from different towns, and the pronunciation of only ten morphemes out of over 3,000 has been found to vary slightly, depending on the town of the speaker.

Traditions and History

According to tradition the Efik originally lived with other Ibibio groups at Idua, a town near the Oron area. The Efik emigrated, or were expelled by other Ibibio, during the first half of the seventeenth century as the result, it is said, of a quarrel concerning an axe borrowed from an Ibibio woman by an Efik woman named Abasi. Abasi broke the axe while chopping firewood and left the broken axe on the ground instead of returning it to the owner or telling her of the damage. The Ibibio woman took the broken axe to Abasi and told her to repair it. Abasi became annoyed and threw the axe into a latrine. When the husband of the Ibibio woman heard of Abasi's atrocious action he wanted to fight the Efik, but Abasi's husband said that the quarrel should be submitted to arbitration by the elders. Abasi remained obdurate before the judges and cursed the Ibibio people, who thereupon attempted to punish her. The Efik came to her defence and, in the fighting which followed, the Ibibio expelled the Efik from the area. Some of the Efik paddled up the Cross River and settled in the Enyong area, where they became known as the Enyong. The other groups paddled down the Cross River and founded Creek Town. Internecine strife at Creek Town caused several families to emigrate and found

[1] Forde and Jones, op. cit., p. 90.

[2] M. D. W. Jeffreys, *Old Calabar and Notes on the Ibibio Language*, 1935.

4   EFIK TRADERS OF OLD CALABAR

Obutong, 'Old Town'. A little later other families from Creek Town migrated to a location near Old Town where they founded Duke Town some time after 1748[1] in order to prevent the domination of the European trade by Old Town, which enjoyed a favourable anchorage for European ships.[2]

When the Efik first settled at Creek Town they found a small village of Efut settlers living in the immediate vicinity. The Efut had originally migrated from the southern Cameroons area and, in the middle of the nineteenth century, still preserved traces of their own language; but at the present time they speak Efik as their mother tongue.

The name Calabar or Old Calabar is not shown on fifteenth- or sixteenth-century Spanish and Portuguese maps, but first appears on Dutch maps of the seventeenth century.[3] Joannis Jansonii mentions Rio Real d'calabar and the towns Calabari and Out Calabar on his map, *Negritarum Regnum* (*c.* 1650). The word Calabar is not of Efik origin; it is believed to have been first applied to the New Calabar River, farther to the west, so-called from the villages of the Kalabari Ijaw who lived along its banks. Through error the name came to be used for the Cross River estuary area, which in turn was later called 'Old' Calabar to distinguish it from 'New' Calabar, a town situated on the Niger River near Bonny, and now known as Degema.[4]

By the beginning of the eighteenth century Old Calabar had become a well-known minor trading centre for slaves. The method of trade formerly practised in the Bight of Biafra was known as 'trust trade' and involved the giving of trade articles by a European trader to a native chief of good reputation, who would use them to purchase a specified quota of

[1] See the testimony of Captain Ambrose Lace before Parliament in 1789, *Abridgement of the Minutes of Evidence* (taken before a Committee of the whole House . . .), No. II, 1790, p. 244.

[2] Other traditions suggest that the colonization of the Cross River estuary was a gradual and complex process involving elements from many eastern Ibibio groups. See Goldie, 1874, p. 357 and Jeffreys, op. cit., pp. 26-32.

[3] P. A. Talbot, *The Peoples of Southern Nigeria*, 1926, I, p. 183.   [4] Ibid.

THE EFIK PEOPLE

slaves. The articles given included such things as copper bars, knives, rum, gin, basins, tankards, beads, locks, mirrors, guns, powder, and shot. Smith[1] remarks: 'Few things astonish a white man so much on a first visit to this place on a trading expedition, as the amount of goods solicited by and entrusted to this people. With the utmost confidence a fellow nearly naked will ask you for three, or four, or even five thousand pounds worth of goods on credit, and individuals are often trusted to that amount. I have trusted more than one man with goods, the returns of which were worth between two and three thousand pounds. Not one in ten however that asks for trust is worthy of credit to the amount of so many farthings. Some few of the chiefs are really splendid merchants. Hard in making their bargains, but strict in their payments they approach very near, in their commercial transactions, to their brethren of Europe and the civilized parts of Asia and America.'

The giving of presents or 'dashes' was also an important aspect of trading and Smith[2] again notes that 'to know how to make presents judiciously is a very important part of the knowledge of it [trading]. When the trader comes to see your goods he asks for a dash; when he brings you goods he wants one; and when he receives payment another. The head slaves look for dashes. The pilots both in bringing you to and taking you out of the rivers, independent of a fixed payment, receive dashes. . . .'

The Efik formerly had a currency of imported copper and iron rods and copper wire. Barbot[3] states that in Calabar, 'The Blacks here reckon by copper bars, reducing all sorts of goods to such bars; for example, one bar of iron, four copper bars; a man slave for thirty-eight; and a woman slave for thirty-seven or thirty-six copper bars.' Crow[4] states, 'The

[1] J. Smith, *Trade and Travels in the Gulph of Guinea*, 1851, p. 187.

[2] Ibid., p. 186.

[3] J. Barbot, *A Description of the Coasts of North and South Guinea* (Vol V. of Churchill's *Voyages*), 1732, p. 383.

[4] H. Crow, *Memoirs of the late Captain Hugh Crow of Liverpool*, 1830, p. 283.

6   EFIK TRADERS OF OLD CALABAR

currency is copper; and the palm oil, a principal commodity, is sold at so many coppers, say at the rate of from eight to twelve for a croo, which is about twelve gallons. The coppers are generally a nominal value, though they are represented occasionally by copper rods.' Talbot[1] gives the value of rods in the early years of the present century as 1s.

In addition to exchanging goods for slaves, all European ships had to pay a duty to Efik chiefs for the privilege of trading. This duty was known as 'comey' or 'coomey', a name which, according to Hutchinson,[2] may be derived from native attempts to pronounce the word 'custom'. Smith,[3] referring to customs duty in the Bight of Biafra, remarks that 'as soon as the ship is safely moored opposite the town, the trader goes on shore to arrange with the king what goods are to be paid as "comey" or custom. The quantity is regulated by the registered tonnage of the ship; you must settle with him the best way you can as to quality. Generally speaking he is not bad to deal with in settling for comey, not half so bad as in his private trade transactions. The profits of the latter are his own; of the former, the country participates.'

In 1852 a conference between British supercargoes and the Efik of Duke Town and Creek Town decreed that comey was to be levied at the rate of twenty coppers per registered ton, and divided as to two-thirds to King Eyo of Creek Town and one-third to King Duke Ephraim of Duke Town.[4] Sometimes there were disputes as to the amount to be paid, as in the letter cited by Williams,[5] written by the chief of Old Town to Ambrose Lace, a Liverpool merchant, in which the chief complains that two European captains attempted to prevent a third from loading his ship at Calabar under the pretext

[1] P. A. Talbot, op. cit., III, p. 876.

[2] T. J. Hutchinson, *Ten Years' Wanderings among the Ethiopians*, 1861, p. 18.

[3] Smith, op. cit., p. 184.   [4] Hutchinson, op. cit., pp. 196-7.

[5] G. Williams, *History of the Liverpool Privateers*, &c., 1897, pp. 524-7.

THE EFIK PEOPLE

that the last should pay the same amount of comey as they had done.

The Efik enslaved those of their own people who were guilty of theft or adultery, and also captured or purchased slaves from neighbouring tribes. A raid undertaken for this purpose is described by Isaac Parker,[1] a ship-keeper who jumped ship in Duke Town in 1765 and remained there for five months. While he was there Dick Ebro asked him to go to war with him, to which he agreed, and they fitted out and armed the canoes and went up the river, 'lying under the bushes in the day when they came near a village, and taking hold of every one they could see. These they handcuffed, brought down to the canoes, and so proceeded up the river, till they got to the amount of 45, with whom they returned to New Town[2] where, sending to the captains of the shipping, they divided them among the ships. About a fortnight after they went again, and were out eight or nine days, plundering other villages higher up the river. They seized on much the same number as before, brought them to New Town, gave the same notice and disposed of them as before among the ships.'

The English of the West Indies regarded slaves from Calabar as rebellious, and preferred slaves from the Gold Coast.[3] Slaves of Efik or Ibibio origin were regarded as exceedingly fierce; in the West Indies they were known as Moko.[4] Liverpool ships obtained from Calabar 2,810 slaves in 1752, 3,050 in 1771, 2,473 in 1798, and 1,654 in 1799.[5] Antera Duke records in his diary a total of 7,511 slaves exported from Calabar in the years 1785-8. Although England attempted to blockade the West African coast in 1807 and

[1] *Abridgement of the Minutes of Evidence* (taken before a Committee of the whole House . . .), III, 1790, pp. 53-4.

[2] Duke Town, see below p. 119.

[3] E. Donnan, *Documents Illustrative of the History of the Slave Trade*, 1930-5, I, p. 108.

[4] C. G. A. Oldendorps, *Geschichte der Mission der Evangelischen Brüder auf den Carabischen Inseln*, 1777.

[5] E. Donnan, op. cit., II, pp. 496-9, 545-6, 642-9.

8 EFIK TRADERS OF OLD CALABAR

afterwards, the slave-trade continued at Calabar until 1841, when British representatives signed anti-slavery treaties with the chiefs of Duke Town and Creek Town.

Before the Church of Scotland Mission was established in 1846 no Europeans had resided in Efik towns for any appreciable length of time. The missionaries[1] started schools, reduced the Efik language to writing and, together with the British Consul, eventually suppressed various Efik customs particularly repugnant to Europeans. For some considerable time before the arrival of the missions, however, a number of Efik had kept business records written in English. Williams[2] gives the contents of several letters, the earliest example being dated 1773, written by Efik in Calabar to Liverpool merchants. Crow[3] remarked that 'at Calabar, the duke and a considerable number of his men can speak tolerably good broken English, and even write mercantile letters sufficiently explicit and intelligible on ordinary affairs. Several of these have been addressed to gentlemen in Liverpool, as well as epistles of a more private and confidential nature, accompanied by presents, in return for others transmitted to the writers. These documents, particularly those of Duke Ephraim, are concise in diction and exhibit a mixture of seriousness and drollery which render them curiosities of their kind.' Smith[4] also comments on the ability of Duke Ephraim and the principal chiefs of Old Calabar to read and write, but the inhabitants of the other rivers 'trust entirely to their memories which necessity and use have enabled them to cultivate and strengthen to an extraordinary degree'.

The Efik acquired many European goods during the two centuries of the slave-trade. Some chiefs possessed European-built two-storey wood houses as early as 1785, as Duke's diary shows. The materials for the houses were sent from Liverpool and they were constructed in Calabar. Several of

[1] D. McFarlan, *Calabar*, provides an excellent history of the Church of Scotland Mission in Calabar Province.

[2] Williams, op. cit., pp. 541-9.   [3] Crow, op. cit., pp. 285-6.

[4] Smith, op. cit., pp. 199-200.

THE EFIK PEOPLE

these houses, although undoubtedly of later construction, still exist in Creek Town and Duke Town. The upper floor, which the Efik, borrowing an English shipboard term, call *dek*, is always of wood. The house of Duke Ephraim, who was chief of Duke Town when Crow was there, is described as being 'of considerable size, raised on pillars from the ground, and the original structure has been of late years much enlarged. . . . This house or place is stocked with numerous clocks, watches, and other articles of mechanism, sofas, tables, pictures, beds, porcelain cabinets, &c. of European manufacture; most of which are huddled together, in confusion, amongst numerous fetiches, and in a state of decay, from disuse, carelessness and want of cleaning.' This blend of the European with the indigenous was also apparent in Duke Ephraim's dress, which, although generally very simple, 'consisting of a paan or mantle, with a sash formed of a white handkerchief or piece of cloth', was on occasions 'of a more gaudy and imposing description', when he would wear 'a sort of robe or mantle reaching to the knee, and composed of several colours, with a silk sash thrown over the shoulder', and 'a gold-laced round hat, like those worn by gentlemen's servants, which is sometimes set off with plumes of feathers'.[1]

Another vivid description of a chief's dress and also of an Efik war canoe is given by Waddell[2] in his account of the 1846 punitive expedition led by Eyamba of Duke Town against Umon, an island in the centre of the Cross River about forty miles from Duke Town. He writes: 'His great canoe was gaily decked out with several ensigns streaming in the wind, British ensigns, with his name thereon in large letters. The little house amidships was brilliantly painted red and yellow. Astride the roof thereof sat two men beating drums with might and main. Before it stood Eyamba, shaded by his grand umbrella, dressed as usual, except in having a gold laced cocked hat under his arm, and a splendid sword,

[1] H. Crow, op. cit., p. 275.

[2] H. M. Waddell, *Twenty-nine Years in the West Indies and Central Africa*, 1863, pp. 286-8.

EFIK TRADERS OF OLD CALABAR

a present from the Dutch Government, at his side. In the bows a large gun pointed forward, and before it stood a man with a bundle of reeds, which he kept shaking at arms length to warn every obstacle and danger out of the way. On each side sat fifteen men with paddles, and between them down the centre stood a row of men armed with cutlasses and guns. The king's body-guard were immediately around him. A train of inferior canoes, ornamented and arranged in the same style, belonging to the lesser gentry, were in his wake.'

The hospitality of the chiefs was on a lavish scale, and it was the custom at Calabar, as at Bonny, for one of the chief's wives to prepare a 'lunch' for the reception of the English and other captains in the port. At the 'neatly laid' table the principal dish would be a yam chop consisting of 'boiled yams and boiled fowl, for here everything is boiled—served up with sweet palm-oil and pepper', which Crow admits that he often ate with a good relish.[1] Waddell[2] writes that 'Eyamba held a weekly feast or levee thereon, and invited his friends, black and white. At two o'clock, a large gun, fired on the beach, summoned the company to dinner. They assembled in the state-room of the iron palace. Eyamba entered dressed in his best style—broad silk waist cloth, hat and feathers, a profusion of beads, but neither shirt nor shoe. He went round shaking hands with every one, and then paraded admiringly before the mirrors, as his manner was.

'In the dining-room a long table was laid out, and properly furnished. Eyamba took the head, his white guests sat all on his right, the black on his left. The foot remained vacant, to be filled as friends arrived. A basin, ewer, and towel were carried round for every one to wash hands, which was done by a little water being *poured* on them in eastern style. Then came in a file of stout girls in native undress, each bearing on her head a large covered calabash, with an ornamental cloth thereon, which she placed on the table. Their contents had a novel appearance. Yams and fish, stewed together with palm oil, vegetables, and pepper,

[1] Crow, op. cit., pp. 273-4.   [2] Waddell, op. cit., pp. 247-8.

filled one; yams and goat flesh, similarly dressed, another, and so on. They looked savoury, and had a fragrant odour, but their appearance was not tempting. A native earthen pot, with rich "black soup", as it was called, accompanied by a dish of pounded yams, or "fufu", held a prominent place.

'Every dish formed a course; and Eyamba helped them all himself, in succession, to all his guests, without asking anyone what he would choose. But we were free to eat much or little, or none at all, as we liked, and send away our plate.' Waddell seems to have been cautious rather than enthusiastic, trying a little of each dish, as he puts it 'more from conscience than curiosity or appetite' and found them 'not unpalatable, though too oily and spicy'. However, the numerous servants and on-lookers, who filled the lower part of the room, eagerly carried off the full plates of the foreigners' leavings, for 'the white gentlemen all ate sparingly; the black enjoyed themselves highly, not over particular in their manners, using their fingers often for forks, and their lips for napkins. The "fufu" was not eaten, but swallowed in great masses. Every one hewed a lump of it, and laid it on the table, beside his plate of "black soup". Rolling a piece, between his hands, into a ball, nearly as large as a hen's egg, he stuck the middle finger of his right hand lightly into it, dipped it into the sauce, then slipped it into his mouth, and over his throat instantly, without chewing. The native nobility performed this feat with an ease which the practice of a lifetime alone could have given, and foreigners in vain tried to imitate. Laughing and joking enlivened the table while discussing this dish, the use of the teeth not hindering the use of the tongue. . . . The drink at this royal feast was *mimbo*, a milky-looking liquor, fresh drawn from a species of palm-tree, of agreeable taste and unintoxicating nature. Eyamba and his gentry drank it from overflowing quart mugs, while tumblers served our side of the table.'

Today Duke Town has grown into a major African port owing to its accessibility to European shipping, for it is now the major component of Calabar Township, which also includes

EFIK TRADERS OF OLD CALABAR

Henshaw Town and Big Qua Town. The present population of Calabar is approximately 125,000, with the indigenous Efik constituting a distinct minority among the influx of Ibibio, Ibo, Yoruba, Hausa, and Upper Cross River tribes.

Creek Town, because of its inaccessibility, has not undergone the same changes, but the population has declined, since educated inhabitants are forced to seek employment elsewhere in Nigeria. Thanks to the education made available by the Church of Scotland Mission, many Efik contributed, at an early date, to the development of modern Nigeria, serving as teachers, physicians, lawyers, and employees of the Government or of European firms.

Occupations and Crafts

Among the Efik, farm preparation begins in January, when men clear and fire the bush, women weed, and both sexes gather the harvest. Crops grown include taro, maize, gourds, melons, peppers, beans, and several varieties of plant leaves, besides yam and manioc, which are the staple foods of the Efik. Food recipes are similar to those of the Ibo and the Yoruba; they refuse to eat snakes, leopards, or owls. The products of the oil-palm tree provide the major export and cash crop.

Hunting is no longer an important occupation, since game is scarce, but men occasionally hunt monkeys and antelope with antiquated fire-arms known as Dane or cap guns and modern shot-guns; game is also trapped. Many men fish either full or part-time, usually working in pairs and travelling in dugout canoes.

All large Efik settlements, like those of neighbouring tribes, possess a market. At the present time the European Sunday has superseded the Efik day on which markets were forbidden. But they still observe an original eight-day week and, when a particular market-day falls on a Sunday, the market is automatically cancelled. Women are the main sellers in the markets, where they retail farm produce and imported European goods; men sometimes sell palm-wine, mats,

THE EFIK PEOPLE

baskets, and cloth, while many engage in wholesale trading between markets; a few surreptitiously smuggle by canoe between the Spanish island of Fernando Po and the Nigerian mainland, obtaining low-cost alcoholic beverages in exchange for yams, palm-oil, and garri.

A few men excel in wood-carving, but there are no specialist carvers. Efik masks have no distinctive style: some are similar to Ibibio masks; others resemble those of the neighbouring Ekoi. The Efik seldom wear masks or carved head-dresses, their use being generally confined to children, who wear masks of Ibibio make. Head-dresses are frequently covered with antelope skin, a practice derived from the Ekoi, who are noted for these.

Formerly gourds were incised with geometrical designs made with a heated stylus. In the 1890's women began to decorate Birmingham brass trays and dishes in relief, using a method similar to the *repoussé* technique. The tray was placed on an inverted mortar and tapped with a small nail to depress the area surrounding the design, and thus make the design stand out in relief. Various geometrical patterns were made which, together with the untapped areas, formed figures of flowers, leaves, guinea-fowl, animals, and persons in costume. At the present time only two women of Duke Town specialize in brass-tapping.

Women also make patchwork cloths, which are used to cover gifts when sending them to friends. The cloths vary in size and colour and consist of a series of different-coloured strips bordering a geometrical design.

Social Life

The domestic unit formerly consisted of the polygynous family, which included a man, his wives, and their offspring, but now, for economic and other reasons, polygyny is relatively infrequent. A larger unit, based on patrilineal kinship, was the *ufɔk*, or 'house', consisting of the male descendants of a recent ancestor and all the slaves they owned. In former times the head of the house was the oldest living male,

14 EFIK TRADERS OF OLD CALABAR

but in the *ufɔk* today the leader is usually selected for his ability. Efik settlements are divided into wards, each corresponding to still larger bodies of patrilineally related men. The Efik use a descriptive kinship terminology in which the eldest son, eldest daughter, second eldest son and second eldest daughter are designated by special terms.

Children inherit the property of the father and mother. The eldest son and eldest daughter receive the greatest share of movable property, the older having the first choice. Heirs rarely divide land, but they share the produce or income derived from it.

Sexual relations and marriage are forbidden between members of the same family, between parallel and cross-cousins, between a man and his wife's mother, sister, or daughter, or the wife of a brother or half-brother even after the brother's death. Intercourse with a father's wife is regarded as adultery and formerly was punished with death or slavery.

On marriage, a series of gifts is made by the groom to the bride and her kin. These include cash to the value of about £12, called *ekebɔ ndɔ* (box of marriage) or *okuk ndɔ* (marriage money). This constitutes the only form of marriage which permits the husband to include the children as members of his lineage, to receive the marriage payment for his daughters, and to punish his wife for adultery. Unlike the other Ibibio groups, the Efik allow the bride to retain a large portion of the marriage payment, which she uses to establish herself in marketing or to purchase necessary household articles. A wife cannot divorce her husband without returning his gifts, except in cases of extreme ill-treatment, threats to her personal safety, or failure to provide for her. If a husband divorces his wife without cause, he forfeits his marriage payment.

The Efik were formerly grouped in age sets, each of which included all men and women born within a one-year period. Certain sets acted as watchmen to prevent attacks of enemy war parties or slave rebellions. Each member of the same age set addresses another member by the reciprocal term *da*, but

THE EFIK PEOPLE

to call a member of an older set by this term would be a grave insult.

Young girls are called *ŋka ifere*, 'age set of nakedness', until the ceremony of dressing them in new cloths, which signifies the attainment of womanhood, is performed. Formerly when a girl was nine to eleven years old her parents placed her in the *ufɔk ŋkuh*, 'house of seclusion' or 'fattening house'. The length of time she remained there depended on the wealth of the father and the status of the girl in her family. The eldest daughter always spent a longer period in seclusion than her sisters. The longer the period of seclusion, the greater the prestige of the girl, since only a wealthy man could afford to keep his daughter inactive for as long as seven years. The average period was three. The practice of secluding girls still obtains, and during the period of seclusion a girl refrains from doing any normal domestic work and is expected to eat as much as she can and to grow fat, for corpulence is a sign of health among the Efik. Every day someone massages her body and rubs ashes on her skin to make the body fleshy and the skin smooth. If a chief or an elderly woman should visit a girl just after she has finished a meal and say they want to see her eat, etiquette demands that she should eat again, even though satiated. Although special relatives and female friends may visit the girl, the family excludes all outsiders so that she may later amaze the village with her beauty. Ideally, a girl in seclusion does not have sexual relations with her intended spouse, for she disgraces herself and her family if she conceives in the fattening house. Efik apply the nickname *ebua*, 'dog', to a girl who has coitus while in seclusion or who marries before undergoing seclusion. Formerly clitoridectomy was performed when a girl first went into seclusion; nowadays it is usually done at the age of three. When a girl comes out of seclusion, her family invites friends and relatives to the ceremony. The guests always bring gifts and money, known as *okuk utuak ndom*, 'money of rubbing chalk', since female attendants rub chalk on the girl's right hand as each donation is made.

EFIK TRADERS OF OLD CALABAR

The free-born and the slaves constituted two distinct classes in Efik society. All children of free-born parents were naturally free; descendants of slaves could acquire free status in the third generation. The free-born possessed many rights and privileges denied to slaves, such as membership in the higher grades of the Leopard Society, and the right to wear certain articles of costume, or to dress in velvet cloth. The free-born usually treated their slaves kindly, provided they were obedient. They rarely sold their personal slaves to Europeans, as they considered this to be a mark of poverty, unless the slaves were guilty of gross disobedience, theft, adultery, or sorcery.

Every major Efik settlement had a senior ɔbɔŋ or chief who always ranked high in the Leopard Society and was usually the head of the highest of its grades in the town. The chief enforced laws in his role as head of the society, mediated or adjudicated in disputes, led armed forces in time of war, and arranged peace pacts with neighbours. In Creek Town, since 1820, the chieftainship has been confined to the lineal descendants of Willy Eyo Honesty, mentioned in Duke's diary.[1]

The Egbo or Leopard Society (see note 2, p. 66) was the most important men's association and consisted of several grades, each possessing a distinctive costume. There were further sub-divisions within the higher grades. Under the aegis of the chief and the important elders of the town, the Leopard Society promulgated and enforced laws, judged important cases, recovered debts, protected the property of members, and constituted the actual executive government of the Efik. It enforced its laws by capital punishment or fines for individuals, and by trade boycotts against European traders or other Efik towns.[2]

Ideally, every Efik settlement should have its own Egbo Society shed or 'palaver house'; that of Duke Town was described by Hutchinson[3] as follows: 'The palaver-house

[1] On chiefship among the Efik, see below, pp. 125-6.

[2] The political functions are discussed by Mr. Jones, see pp. 140-4 below.

[3] Hutchinson, *Impressions of Western Africa*, 1858, pp. 119-20.

THE EFIK PEOPLE

consists of two walls running parallel for about forty yards, terminated by a transverse wall, about as many feet in length, and thatched with a stout bamboo roof. The end by which it is entered is opened from side to side, a space of nearly eighteen inches intervenes between the tops of the walls running lengthways and the roof; and there is an ascent from the road by half-a-dozen steps to the floor, which is hard and smooth. In the centre of the entrance is a huge hollow brass pillar reaching up to the roof; further in are two more of equally imposing diameter, whilst between them are a large bell and a piece of wood. The latter is drum-like in shape, with a slit longitudinally in it, and fixed to the pillar. This is the Egbo drum which is beaten to alarm the inhabitants in case of a fire, to give notice of the attack of an enemy, or to signify the fact of a leopard having been captured, each occurrence being indicated by a peculiarity of beating the drum, which is known as soon as the sound is heard. In the farthest corner of the house is a private sanctuary into which none but the privileged are admitted on occasions of Egbo meetings, and outside the front are two flourishing ju-ju trees, with five pillars of stone before them, said to be solidified basaltic lava brought from Prince's Island, and erected there to the memory of five sovereigns of Old Kalabar.'

The society possesses a plot of land known as *ikɔt ekpe*, 'bush of the Leopard Society', where members don costumes and observe ceremonies safe from the intrusion of the un-initiated who never dare enter the precincts. In the bush of Creek Town there was formerly a large tree from which con-victed murderers were compelled to hang themselves. The society's costumed figure, *Idem Ikwɔ*, wears a bell tied on his hip and carries a whip; the tinkling of the bell announces his approach to all the uninitiated, who flee from him if they desire to escape being whipped. He is always accompanied by members of the society to the society's bush, where he takes off his costume. Sometimes the Efik pretended that the leopard figure had escaped and members hurried hither and thither attempting to locate and capture him.

18 EFIK TRADERS OF OLD CALABAR

The roar of a leopard is simulated by a secret noise-making apparatus called *mbɔk*. Whenever the Leopard men produce the noise they always curtain off the room with blue and white Ibo-dyed *ukara* cloth and hang the leaf of the *Newbouldia laevis* tree on the curtain to prevent the entrance of un-authorized persons. Manipulators of the mechanism produce the tones of names, &c., thus enabling the mechanism to 'talk' in a manner analogous to drum signals. The apparatus (which is not a bull-roarer) is regarded as particularly sacred.

Another important men's secret association is *Ɔbɔn* which formerly possessed five grades, of which only two now exist. The *Ɔbɔn* is regarded as a 'brother' to the Leopard Society, and functions primarily as a burial society which honours deceased members with a ceremony during the memorial activities.

A secret association known as *Ekpri Akata* meets at night in November, December, and January to sing songs accompanied by drums, and to report gossip to the villagers. Members disguise their voices by means of a small mechanism, and can also produce noises imitating a dog, cow, toad, bee, and crying baby.

Folklore, Musical Instruments, and Signal Drums

Efik folklore includes tales, proverbs, riddles, tone riddles, stereotyped expressions of sarcasm, a form of poetry, curses, songs, greetings, and special forms of commemoration. Folk-tales are numerous and include the Uncle Remus type of animal story in which the tortoise is the trickster.[1] Ordinary riddles are not as numerous as proverbs which, with folk-tales, constitute the most common folklore forms. Tone riddles consist of a question and an answer, both of which have identical or very similar tone patterns although differing in morphemes. The tone riddle is used as a form of amusement, greeting, explanation for an action, indirect

---

[1] See H. Cobham, 'Animal Stories from Calabar', *J. Afr. Soc.*, IV, 1904, pp. 307-9; J. C. Cotton, 'Calabar Stories,' ibid., V, 1906, pp. 191-6; E. Dayrell, *Folk Stories from Southern Nigeria*, 1910.

THE EFIK PEOPLE

method of cursing, and an erotic *double entendre* between the sexes.

The Efik have several types of single-membrane drums, one of which is a circular kettle-like drum supported on three legs and used only by members of the Ɔbɔn society. A trumpet made of a bamboo tube decorated with red cloth is blown in 'medicine' sheds when sacrifices are made.

Messages are sent by means of the wooden 'signal-drum', the double-headed iron gong, and the trumpet. These devices reproduce, with occasional slight modifications, the tone phonemes of proverbs or nicknames which possess stereotyped meanings when heard as drum signals. The signal-drum is really a slit-gong constructed from a hollowed log in such a manner that two lips of the exterior surface converge over the hollowed portion. A large signal-drum is capable of sending messages receivable within a radius of five to seven miles. Other drummers relay the messages to their destination. At the present time the signal-drum is only used during a period of mourning to send messages of condolence to the bereaved and messages of defiance to enemies of the deceased. The Leopard Society possesses a special drum, on which secret signs are painted (see note 43, p. 71, below).

Beliefs and Cults

These include belief in a Supreme God, in the power of ancestors and other supernatural beings, in magic-medicine, soul-affinity with animals, reincarnation, sorcery, and witchcraft. Aboriginal observances consist in showing proper respect to the Supreme God, in abstaining from such evils as adultery, murder, theft, false witness, and work on the day sacred to God, and in offering sacrifices to magic-medicines, supernatural powers, and the ancestors.

The Efik call their Supreme God *Abasi*, and often use the expression *Etenyin Abasi*, 'our father God'. *Abasi* is the only deity in the universe; he dwells somewhere in the sky, he created the world and discountenances all injustice and evil.

c

20 EFIK TRADERS OF OLD CALABAR

On the one day of the eight-day week which was sacred to *Abasi*, the Efik did not hold markets, hunt, fish, or beat drums.

There is belief in reincarnation, and if a child resembles a deceased relative the family considers the child to be a reincarnation of that relative. A concept known as *akaŋa* (vow) postulates that before birth an individual promises God what he will be and do after he is born, whether he will be prosperous or poor, and how many years he intends to live. When the individual is born he must fulfil his promise. *Enye akpa uyo akaŋa abasi*, 'He dies from promise to God', is an Efik saying frequently heard when any one dies either early in life or just after becoming wealthy.

In earlier times it was thought that every individual possessed an *ukpɔŋ* or 'soul' which lived in a particular animal in the bush. Whatever happened to the animal affinity also happened at the same time and in the same way to the human being whose affinity the animal was.[1] A very powerful person would have a chimpanzee as his animal affinity, a slow person a python.

Supernatural powers (*ndem*) inhabit large trees, stone outcroppings, pools, and parts of the Calabar River. Each Efik town possesses a particular supernatural power which protects it and to which the townspeople offer sacrifices.

Certain powerful medicines, *ibɔk* and *mbiam*, manufactured by man derive their potency from their ingredients. *Mbiam* is a magically potent liquid used in swearing oaths, which causes anyone who swears falsely to swell up, sicken, and die. *Ibɔk* are classifiable into two types: medicinal and magical. Medicinal *ibɔk* are used to cure disease, while magical *ibɔk* are used to ensure good fortune or to prevent bad fortune, as love medicines, and to injure or destroy enemies. Although held to be equally powerful, *mbiam* and *ibɔk* are believed to work in different ways. *Ibɔk* acts without mercy and does exactly what the person who makes it desires, but *mbiam*

[1] Some Efik believe that the Nigerian Government prohibited the hunting of the manatee (as a conservation measure) because Europeans possess the manatee as an animal affinity.

THE EFIK PEOPLE

never harms an innocent person and always shows some sign before it acts, so that the person will know that something is wrong. Such signs may be a forest bird building a nest in a house, a white vulture, or a rare kind of giant millipede.

An example of magical medicine is *ibɔk usiak owo*, 'medicine for mentioning persons', resorted to by a husband who suspects his wife of adultery and desires to learn the name of the guilty man. This medicine also prevents a woman from giving birth until she has named her adulterous partner. The leaf of a species of *Dracaena* tree, together with fibre from a wine-palm tree, bark of *Albizzia zygia*, and a small croaker fish, are cooked in a pot until the mixture turns black. Then the root of the *Urera manii* plant is added, and the mixture is put into a sheepskin bag. The bag is placed under the door or pillow. While the wife sleeps the medicine will make her mention the names of all the men with whom she has had sexual relations, but the husband must stay awake to prevent the medicine from affecting him.

Two types of sorcery or witchcraft, called by the Efik *ifɔt*, are believed to exist: white and black. 'White' witchcraft only defends people against the possessors of 'black' witchcraft who cause harm. Any adult may become possessed of black witchcraft and cause death, sickness, or loss of wealth to his neighbours and relatives. Witches form a society and meet at night to cause mischief; they are red in colour because they are in the habit of removing their skins, which they leave at home to deceive people into thinking that they are asleep, while they themselves appear outside in their raw flesh. They can attract money to themselves, and a rainbow signifies that a witch is drinking money from the house at the end of the rainbow.

There is a special witch society called *unam okuk*, literally 'animal of money', but translated by the Efik as 'money medicine society', membership of which is obtained either by sacrificing a close relative or by handing over his material wealth. If a witch pledges a person's wealth to the witch society, none of his relatives will suffer, but the person will

22   EFIK TRADERS OF OLD CALABAR

lose his wealth through accident; after he has lost his money seven times he will become wealthy. Although the Efik aver that the *unam okuk* society was introduced from the upper Cross River, indigenous Efik witchcraft beliefs contained essentially similar features.

The Efik believe that the *esere* or Calabar bean (*Physostigma venemosum*) possesses the power to reveal and destroy witchcraft.[1] A suspected person is given eight of the beans ground and added to water as a drink. If he is guilty, his mouth shakes and mucus comes from his nose. His innocence is proved if he lifts his right hand and then regurgitates. If the poison continues to affect the suspect after he has established his innocence, he is given a concoction of excrement mixed in water which has been used to wash the external genitalia of a female. If a person dies from the ordeal his body is usually thrown into the forest, after the eyes have been removed. A type of clay pot called *eso ntibe*, which has several holes and is normally used for drying shrimps, is put over its head. Corpses of witches were sometimes buried with the face to the ground, or the corpse was burnt and the ashes buried. In this way the Efik hoped to prevent the return of the *ekpo ifɔt* or 'witch ghost' to hinder and 'wreak havoc' among the living. If trouble continues to occur in a compound, the people may suspect a recently deceased relative of being an undetected witch. The relatives exhume the corpse to inspect the process of decay. If it appears fresh, with little sign of decay, the deceased is believed to have been a witch and the corpse is burnt.

There are important observances connected with burial and mourning. The dead are buried within the compound in one of the rooms of the house. The Efik say that they do it in this way to prevent enemies from cutting off the head to use it for magical purposes. The 'mourning house' (*ufɔk ikpo*) consists of relatives and friends who sleep on mats in the

---

[1] Nigerian law forbids the *esere* ordeal, but occasional cases still occur when individuals desire to show their innocence of any imputation of witchcraft.

THE EFIK PEOPLE

compound. At dawn the women awaken and wail for about an hour, after which they disperse about their daily routine, reassembling in the evening. This aspect of mourning generally lasts for one month, during which friends and relatives send food to the 'mourning house' to feed the guests.

Until the termination of the *ikpo*, widows went into a special mourning called *mbukpisi*, during which they ate with wooden spoons, used a piece of calabash as a plate, never combed their hair, wore raffia cloth around the waist, and rubbed cow-dung on their faces and bodies every morning as a sign of sorrow.

After the *ikpo* period ended, various native 'plays' were performed. Finally, the ceremony of *utim udi*, 'pounding the grave', took place. This consisted of excavating the grave to a depth of three to four feet. Friends and relatives assembled about ten o'clock in the morning and danced on the excavated portion of the grave to the accompaniment of songs and the beat of drums. During the day, the earth which had been dug out was put back into the grave a little at a time and trampled by the dancers. The ceremony, which is still observed, usually ends in the late afternoon when the grave is completely re-filled. *Utim udi* must be observed for the parent who died first before it can be held for the other deceased parent, in order to prevent the ghost of the offended parent from causing misfortune to the family.

According to Mr. E. O. Ndem, the climax of mourning was to cry in the town. A procession led by the chief wife of the dead man went from his house to the palaver shed. Members of the extended family followed the widows in the procession, and were followed by female representatives of other extended families. Persons descended from free-born parents moved in rhythm with the drumming, while those who had only one free-born parent hopped on the right or left leg, according to whether the free-born parent was the father or mother. In the palaver shed, or *efe ekpe*, the chief wife of the dead man led the demonstration of mourning, known as *eyet aŋwa*, 'tears outside'. In another form of *eyet aŋwa* the relatives dressed themselves in a special manner and paraded about the town.

24   EFIK TRADERS OF OLD CALABAR

Each individual wore three brass anklets on each leg, and three ivory wristlets on each arm. Women dressed their hair to make three tufts stick up from the head, while men parted their hair into three portions. Women wore velvet arm-bands decorated with beads round the upper arm, and hung three special long beads, front and back, from the string worn around the neck. Both men and women wore small loin-cloths round the waist. One man, dressed in a special costume called *ɔnyɔny*, made of velvet, held a small plaited sacrifice-basket, in which there were various kind of food, plus a small live black chick, and carried a broad-headed walking-stick. Each person held in the left hand a plate containing chalk, and as the procession walked in pairs someone walked up and down rubbing the chalk over each person's head and body. While one person beat a gong slowly, another spoke praises of the dead through a speaking-trumpet. The procession went outside twice, from 3 a.m. to 8 a.m., and from 3 p.m. to 6 p.m. These times were chosen so that everyone in the village would be at home and able to hear what was said about the dead man.

Creek Town last observed *eyet aŋwa* in 1922 during the installation of a chief. Although ex-slaves and free-born contributed towards the ceremony, the free-born decided to observe *eyet aŋwa*. When the ex-slaves saw the ceremony they felt insulted, and poured out the water from the cooking-pots, loosed the cows awaiting slaughter, and ate the food and drank the wine without sharing it with the free-born. After the installation the chief made peace with the slaves; he called them together, asked their forgiveness, gave them wine, food, and a cow, and justified their actions.

Formerly when an important Efik died his relatives con-cealed the news of his death from the townspeople. The corpse was wrapped in a mat and buried in a room in the house; the family and other members of the compound acted as if nothing were the matter, although the widows went into special mourning in their part of the compound. If any enquiries were made about the deceased the relatives said he

THE EFIK PEOPLE

was on a trading expedition. Six months to a year after the burial the death would be announced by beating a signal-drum on the top of the house roof. The townspeople rushed to hear the news when they heard the signal-drum. The mourning observances began from the day the news of the death was officially announced and lasted until the day of the public burial. A platform known as *mkpoto* was built, on which was placed a large wood coffin decorated with cloth and feathers. Relatives and friends came to the compound and gave the deceased his last gifts, such as pieces of cloth, boxes of money, plates, spoons, bars of soap, and similar things. The family pretended that the empty coffin held the corpse and, while reserving the gifts of money to defray the expenses of the mourning period, placed all other gifts in the coffin, which they subsequently buried inside the compound.

An *ɔbɔŋ* ('king' or 'town chief') was always buried secretly in the bush by a few high-ranking members of the Leopard Society, and the location of the grave was never revealed. When the chief died they carried the corpse at night into the bush and dug a grave twenty feet deep. At the bottom an *ada* or tunnel was dug for almost twenty yards and served as a burial chamber. At least four slaves were left alive in the tunnel, usually the personal attendants of the deceased who carried his snuff-box, gun, lantern, and machet. The coffin was placed on the slaves and the grave, except for the tunnel shaft at the bottom, was refilled.

If a person died from tuberculosis, dropsy, or elephantiasis, or if a woman died during pregnancy or childbirth without expelling the foetus, the *ŋkɔ* society, composed solely of men, supervised the burial. The corpse was rolled in a mat and buried at midnight. A society member used a knife tied to a piece of bamboo to cut open the uterus and remove the foetus, or to cut open the peritoneal cavity in a case of dropsy. After the burial the society returned with its juju (usually a drum surmounted by a human skull over which powerful medicine had been rubbed) to the compound of the deceased, where they beat drums, sang, and carried the juju into all the

26 EFIK TRADERS OF OLD CALABAR

rooms of the compound. They also sprinkled protective medicine in all the rooms after cutting a hole in the roof to serve as an exit for evil things. Two plantain stems were placed at right angles to the path to warn everyone that the society was meeting at the house. On the morning following the ceremony ashes from the cooking fire were sprinkled on the two plantain stems and the ceremony officially ended. The Efik believe the *ŋkɔ* juju to be so powerful that the mere sight of it will cause a non-member to sicken and die. Consequently, a father initiates his young son into the society to circumvent any danger. Any food or water which remains in the house during the *ŋkɔ* ceremony is thrown out the following day. Women and non-members who remain in the compound during the ceremony lie on their sides facing the wall with their eyes closed and their heads covered with a blanket.

A ceremony called *ndɔk*, which seems formerly to have had some connexion with the spirits of the dead, was held in November or early December. About a week before the ceremony decorations made from the fresh leaves of the oil-palm tree were tied to the house or compound doorway. Children made *naebikim*, 'scarecrows' or effigies of men and animals, from dried plantain leaves tied around small sticks. On the night reserved for *ndɔk* everyone in the village beat drums, gongs or bottles and shouted '*ekpo ka* (ghosts go!)' to scare out of the town the ghosts of people who had died during the past year. All the decorations and effigies were carried to the beach and thrown in the river. Then most people bathed their feet or bodies in the water to wash off the dirt of the old year.

Nowadays the ceremony of *ndɔk* is held on New Year's Eve under the name *ubin isua*, 'driving the year', but boys do not make effigies for this. They do, however, make *naebikim* effigies for the *mbre judas*, 'Judas play', on Good Friday. The boys put the effigies in front of their houses and at 3 p.m. begin to beat them with sticks, shouting 'Judas killed Christ.'

THE DIARY (1785-8) OF
ANTERA DUKE[1]

IN A MODERN ENGLISH VERSION

18.1.1785

ABOUT 6 a.m. I was at Aqua Landing (Big Beach);[1a] it was a fine morning so I walked with the Ekpe[2] men to Etutim's [house]. So he dash (gave)[3] us one rod[4] and one small case of bottle brandy. Soon afterwards we got all the Ekpe men to go to the Ekpe bush[5] to make bob[6] about (discuss) the Egbo Young[7] and Little Otto[8] palaver.[9] Egbo Young paid one goat and 4 rods and Little Otto paid 4 rods.[10] All the Ekpe men came down to discuss matters with Duke[11] and joined together to put money for 20 men. In all 64 men put money, 45 for Duke's family and 19 for another family.[12]

21.1.1785

At 5 a.m. at Aqua Landing; a fine morning so I went to Captain Savage to get goods [to be exchanged] for slaves.[13]

25.1.1785

About 4 a.m. I went to Eyo Willy Honesty's[14] house and we walked up to see Willy Honesty in his yard.[15] So he killed a big goat for us.[16] Soon after we walked up to see our town[17] and took one great gun[18] to put in a canoe for two of Egbo Young's men to bring home to Aqua Landing. So we went together to Henshaw Town[19] and came back; and at 3 o'clock [after]noon we and everybody went to dash Eyo Willy Honesty's daughter. . . . 1496 rods besides cloth, gunpowder, and iron.[20] So we played[21] all day until night.

28.1.1785

About 6 a.m. at Aqua Landing; a fine morning so I worked in my small yard. At 2 o'clock afternoon we two go aboard

28 EFIK TRADERS OF OLD CALABAR

Captain Small's[22] [ship] with three slaves. So he takes two and we came back.

29.1.1785

About 6 a.m. and a fine morning; so I worked in my small yard all morning and at 2 o'clock [after]noon we went to Captain Brown to take goods for slaves and came back.

30.1.1785

About 6 a.m. at Aqua Landing; a foggy morning, so I was going to work in my little yard, but at the same time we and Tom Aqua and John Aqua joined together to catch men.[23]

2.2.1785

About 6 a.m. at Aqua Landing and a very foggy morning, so I was going to work in my little yard. After that Duke and all of us went to King Ekpe to share Ekpe money for 40 men.[24] After that we came away.

5.2.1785

About 6 a.m. at Aqua Landing with a little morning fog, so I went down to the landing; after . . . noon we three went to Egbo Young's house 'Liverpool Hall'[25] to share three kegs of gunpowder. Soon we hear the news that a ship is coming up [the river] so we run for the landing to get five guns ready to fire. At the same time we see a little canoe coming and he tells us he is Captain Loosdam's tender.

14.2.1785

About 5 a.m. at Aqua Landing with a great morning fog; so I saw my Boostam[26] yam canoe coming home with yams. So I gave Captain Savage 1,000 yams for 100 copper [rods] and at midnight Captain Brown's tender goes away with 430 slaves.

15.2.1785

About 6 a.m. at Aqua Landing with a little morning fog;

THE DIARY OF ANTERA DUKE

so we go on board Captain Loosdam's tender and come back. At 10 o'clock afternoon we hear that Loosdam's tender has gone away with 230 slaves.

23.2.1785

... I go on board Captain Loosdam to break book (make an agreement)[27] for three slaves. So I make an agreement for one slave with Captain Savage and I take goods for slaves from Captain Brown and come back.

6.3.1785

About 6 a.m. at Aqua Landing with a fine morning, so we make all the Ekpe men and Egbo Young go to Henshaw Town to get Ekpe money. At two o'clock afternoon Duke sends his wife to call us. She says that Captain Loosdam has sent his mate to tell Duke about a new ship coming. So I and Esin[28] go aboard Captain Loosdam to find out. So we see the new ship's mate on board and we ask him where the ship is. He says in Parrot Island,[29] so we come ashore and at 7 o'clock at night all the Ekpe men come back. They say that Henshaw Town has put money for 19 men, Cobham Town[30] for 5 men, and one for the Guinea Company[31] Ekpe.

7.3.1785

About 6 a.m. at Aqua Landing with a fine morning, so I go down to the landing. After 10 a.m. we go chop (have a meal) at Egbo Young's house 'Liverpool Hall' and after 12 noon the new ship's mate comes to tell us that he will not come here but go to Cameroons. So Duke says, 'Very well, go away please.'[32]

12.3.1785

About 6 a.m. in Aqua Landing, and a very rainy morning; so I go down with Esin to see Duke in his palaver house. Then we get Willy Honesty to meet at Duke's house with all the gentlemen to discuss the business of the new ship's captain. So we write to ask him to come ashore, but he says he will not

30 EFIK TRADERS OF OLD CALABAR

come ashore. Then we three go aboard his ship to ask him and his answer is that he will not stay in our river. So we come ashore and tell all the gentlemen, and they say: 'Very well, he may go away, please go.'

23.3.1785

At 5 a.m. at Aqua Landing with a fine morning; so I went to see Duke in his yard. We took all our yams and rods for Ekpe yams for the Guinea Company to share. Soon after the Duke got his life [saved] from powder because of his yellow wife Pip.[33] So all of us go to dash him coppers for that. At the same time we see that the small Bristol ship is coming again.

11.4.1785

At 5 a.m. at Aqua Landing with a fine morning; so I go down to the landing. I see nothing all day but at 7 o'clock at night I see two of my people come that I had sent to find Ephraim[34] Aqua Bakassey and they say that the canoe overturned in water and everything is lost including the canoe.[35]

12.4.1785

At 6 a.m. at Aqua Landing with a fine morning, so I walk up the market path and come down to see Duke. Soon after we hear that Duke blew Ekpe[36] on one of his sons named Egbo Abasi, but that son does not obey Ekpe; so we went to the Ekpe Bush to call Ekpe to come and we killed one of his mother's goats.

21.4.1785

At 5 a.m. at Aqua Landing with a fine morning; so at 12 o'clock noon we three go aboard the Brown. We beg him to 'trust' for slaves (see note 13) but he will not. After that we come back. Esin Duke came home from Orroup[37] with seven slaves, and my fisherman came home with slaves and Robin sent me one girl and my first boy came from Curcock[38] with slaves and at midnight we went to Savage's [ship].

THE DIARY OF ANTERA DUKE

22.4.1785

At 5 a.m. in Coffee Duke's canoe we came alongside Captain Savage. So we got together to settle everything we owed him and he gave Crim one very big gun and dash us. So we came away and he left for Parrot Island.

30.4.1785

About 6 a.m. at Aqua Landing; there was a little morning rain, so I got all the Captains to come ashore. I was a little sick so I did not drink any mimbo[39] all day. Before night I heard that Coffee Duke had killed a goat for Egbo Young and Crim's 'play'.

9.5.1785

At 5 a.m. at Aqua Landing; a fine morning so I go down to the landing. After that I see Duke make doctor[40] for his god basin.[41] Soon after we have a very rainy day.

10.5.1785

. . . so I went to work at my cabin. After that I saw Sam Ambo[42] carrying the Ekpe drum[43] to Dick Ephraim, because Ephraim Watt has sent [a message] to Dick Ephraim to pay what he owes concerning Captain Morgan, but I stopped them.

14.5.1785

About 6 a.m. at Aqua Landing; a fine morning, so Duke sent to call us to go to Crim's house to see what he paid to Cameroon Backsider Bakassey for slaves, 560 coppers for all. So they 'chopped doctor' about whether we get slaves for Duke. So we made one canoe carry them home. All the Obong[44] men went to Willy Honesty's Town.[45]

24.5.1785

About 6 a.m. and a fine morning, so I go down to the landing to go aboard Captain Combesboch, I and Esin and Egbo Young. We hear news about a new ship but do not believe it.

32 EFIK TRADERS OF OLD CALABAR

25.5.1785

At 5 a.m. at Aqua Landing and a fine morning; Duke sends to call us to come about Captain Osatam wanting to go away. Soon after Duke and all of us go to Ephraim Offiong's[46] cabin to make doctor (sacrifice) to the old Calabar doctor (?) with a goat; at 3 o'clock afternoon we see that Captain Opter has arrived and we hear that Sam Cooper is in Seven Fathoms Point so we three go down to our canoes.

26.5.1785

At 5 a.m. at Aqua Landing; a fine morning so I go down to the landing. Afterwards I come up to work at my cabin. Soon after I see Esin Duke bringing a new Captain with him to my cabin. He is Captain Combesboch and he says his ship is at Parrot Island. So we three dressed as white men and went down for his boat and one big canoe to bring [his ship] up [the river].[47]

1.6.1785

About 5 a.m. at Aqua Landing and a fine morning. I see Duke's son run to tell us that the Andony[48] people are catching wives and won't let any market [canoes] go past but want to stop men because of the Old Town palaver. So I send Esin down to the landing and Esin gets his canoe and I get Coffee Duke. So we go down in two great canoes and Egbo Young's little canoe and two of Cobham's little canoes. Soon afterwards we see them at Seven Fathoms Point. So they run and my canoe being first runs at them and they get away into the bush. So my canoe gets there at the same time, and [my] people run into the bush and catch one man and two slaves and I take [them in] the canoe. So Esin's canoe catches one man, Egbo Young's canoe and Ephraim Coffee's brother catch one man. So we come home. After we get to town we make Ebrow Opter's cousin go to look for the seven men in the bush.

2.6.1785

At 5 a.m. at Aqua Landing and a fine morning; so I go to

THE DIARY OF ANTERA DUKE

the landing. Afterwards we went to Duke. Duke had a talk with Bakassey and at 9 o'clock two new Captains came ashore. So we went on board the Opter with seven canoes to arrange about comey (duty) (see p. 6). Awaw [the writer's wife] came home with a dead slave from Orrup.

8.6.1785

About 6 a.m. at Aqua Landing; so we go on board the Cooper and come ashore about 8 having taken comey. Soon after we three send to see Eyo Willy Honesty about his not drinking doctor.[49] We three send him three jars of brandy. After 9 o'clock at night Esin Duke comes and tells me that Archibong[50] Duke's sister named Mbong is dead. She was sick for eight days.

9.6.1785

At 5 a.m. we went to Archibong Duke's yard and got people to make a grave in the same yard (see p. 22). After 10 o'clock we put her in the ground and fired three great guns. We see Willy Honesty come to collect comey on board the Opter and Cooper.[51]

15.6.1785

About 5 I was lying in my bed when I heard Egbo Young call out for me; so we three go aboard the Cooper. I get goods for 50 slaves for us three. Soon after we come back.

17.6.1785

At 5 a.m. at Aqua Landing; it was a fine morning, so I go on board the Cooper and come ashore. I make an agreement for two slaves with Captain Osatam. After 9 o'clock at night I sent 5 of my people to go to Yellow Belly's daughter, the mother of Dick Ebrow's sister, to stop one of her house women from giving [any slaves] to the ship, because her brother gave one of my fine girls, which I gave to my wife, to Captain Fairweather[52] who did not pay me. So that made me stop.

34 EFIK TRADERS OF OLD CALABAR

18.6.1785

At 5 a.m. at Aqua Landing and a fine morning, so I go down to the landing after I had made doctor (see note 40) with one goat at my father's basin.

19.6.1785

At 5 a.m. at Aqua Landing; a fine morning, so I go down to the landing; it was a very bad Sunday[53] because of what we owe Captain Tatam. Afterwards I go on board the Cooper.

20.6.1785

At 5 a.m. at Aqua Landing; it was a fine morning, so I go on board the Cooper and then come ashore, and I stop all day; from before 3 o'clock I did not eat anything until night. I gave a jug of brandy and 4 calabashes of food to Archibong's sister's cry (mourning) house.[54]

21.6.1785

At 6 a.m. at Aqua Landing; it was a fine morning, so I go on board the Cooper and Esin goes on board the Combesboch. We come ashore at 3 o'clock after noon. I sent a pound with Esin to give Combesboch to get 8 slaves to pay Captain Tatam. So I paid Tatam for all I owe him and at 7 o'clock I sent my brother Egbo Young to Boostam to trade for slaves.

22.6.1785

About 5 a.m. at Aqua Landing and a fine morning; we saw that Captain Tatam was dropping down to . . . Parrot Island.

23.6.1785

At 5 a.m. at Aqua Landing and a fine morning, so we take Duke down to Tatam, I and Abasi Offiong in one canoe, Esin in one canoe, Duke in one canoe. All the Captains went down, so we get on board at 1 o'clock. Soon after 3 o'clock we leave Duke on board and come back with Tatam himself and all the Captains.

THE DIARY OF ANTERA DUKE 35

24.6.1785

At 5 a.m. at Aqua Landing and a fine morning, so we go on board the Combesboch. We get slaves to ransom Duke's pawn and some to ransom Ephraim Watt's and Ephraim Aqua's pawns. So we go down with Tom Cooper and the Captain of the Combesboch tender and we get on board at 2 o'clock and settle everything and he gave Duke and us 143 kegs of powder, and 984 coppers besides . . . 3 pieces of pocket Honesty (handkerchiefs)[55] for us four and Duke. So we come ashore.

27.6.1785

About 6 a.m. at Aqua Landing and a fine morning; so I get Abasi Cameroon Backsider and one of his boys to take pawns to the ship, and I went on board the Cooper to give pawns and I gave him some goods and we drank all day. Before night Captain Tatam went away with 395 slaves.

29.6.1785

At 4 a.m. we went with a play[56] to Archibong Duke's yard because his sister had died. So he killed a goat for us and after 10 o'clock in the morning we had the Ekpe run. At the same time I saw Egbo Young coming to call me and I found him. Afterwards he said that young Tom Robin was dead after being sick for seven days. My brother Hogan[57] and Archibong Duke's son went to Orroup.

7.7.1785

About 6 a.m. at Aqua Landing; it was a fine morning so I went down to the landing and after 10 o'clock I went on board Captain Collins to ask him why his mate was dropping down [the river]. He says that Captain Combesboch begged him to stay a little longer because he wants to get some pawns out. So I took 2 jars of brandy for myself and Esin and I sent Opter Antera to Enyong[58] to trade for slaves.

11.7.1785

About 6 a.m. at Aqua Landing; it was a very rainy morning.

D

36   EFIK TRADERS OF OLD CALABAR

Captain Collins went over the river bar with 230 slaves and at 1 o'clock we went to Aqua[59] about King Aqua eating new yams. So we four carried him four jugs of brandy as a present and he killed two goats for us and four calabashes of chop. Egbo Young and Esin went home before we came home at 10 o'clock at night.

19.7.1785

At 5 a.m. at Aqua Landing; there was a little morning rain. We hear that Tom Robin's family[60] have cut men's heads off for young Tom. After 10 o'clock we, Duke and all the Captains go down about Captain Brivon's business. After 4 o'clock we see one new ship coming up, so we go aboard it. It is Captain Hughes come up at Seven Fathoms Point.

23.7.1785

About 5 a.m. at Aqua Landing; there was a little morning rain. I have the Cooper carpenter working for me. Soon after I see all the Captains come ashore to take us on board, so all of us go with the King on board Captain Fairweather to collect comey.

3.8.1785

At 5 a.m. at Aqua Landing and a fine morning. So we went in Duke's yard to discuss the dispute between Coffee Sam Ephraim and his wife. Coffee Sam Ephraim's sister came and fought with her brother's wife, and Duke and all of us were damn angry about that fight.

4.8.1785

At 5 a.m. at Aqua Landing and a fine morning, so I go down to the landing. We see Jock Bakassey come to the landing with the Grand Ekpe[61] in a canoe. After a little time we go down with two of Egbo Young's drums to fetch up and carry Ekpe to the bush, and at 7 o'clock at night I have all the Captains to supper at my house.[62]

THE DIARY OF ANTERA DUKE

14.8.1785

At 5 a.m. at Aqua Landing and a fine morning, so I made 6 calabashes of Ekpe chop.[63] Soon after 4 o'clock we carried the Ekpe money to Duke's palaver house to share it among all the old Ekpe men. I put money for three men, Esin Duke put money for three men, Egbo Young for two men, Ephraim Aqua for one man, Hogan Antera for one man. We have heavy rain all night.

29.8.1785

At 6 a.m. at Aqua Landing; there is a little morning rain. So I go on board the Fairweather to fetch his joiner to make windows[64] for my big house. We have a bad Sunday because Egbo Young Offiong is not well.

30.8.1785

At 5 a.m. at Aqua Landing and a fine morning, so I go to see Egbo Young because of his sickness. I have the joiner working for me all day. We have supper with all the Captains at Esin's house.

8.9.1785

About 6 a.m. at Aqua Landing and a fine morning, so I go on board ship and come back. I gave King Up Tabow (?) besides chop, and I killed a goat and gave him and his people about 30 coppers besides mimbo and brandy. So they played all day until night. I made Robert Enyong's father's house drink doctor (see note 49) with Robert and sent him to trade at Enyong. All Cobham town gives Ekpe money for 12 New Town Ekpe, 4 for Guinea Company and Old Town Ekpe.

18.9.1785

About 6 a.m. at Aqua Landing; it was a fine morning, so I went down to the landing. I went on board the Cooper and found Egbo Young. He tells me that not one Captain is aboard for all have gone down to catch fish with Willy Tom Robin. So we come ashore soon afterwards and Esin came to eat with me and drink mimbo.

EFIK TRADERS OF OLD CALABAR

26.9.1785

About 6 a.m. at Aqua Landing; it was a fine morning so I went down to the landing and after 5 o'clock Esin and I went on board the Opter but Esin went away before me. At the same time I and Captain Opter saw one ship coming up from Seven Fathoms Point. Soon we came ashore and I ran to tell Captain Fairweather. So we go down to the landing and get a canoe to go down with Captains Fairweather, Hughes, Combesboch, Opter, and Williams.[65] After 7 o'clock at night all five captains get on board with us. He is Captain Overton and tender for Captain Fairweather. Soon after we came up the river and came ashore to supper at my house with those Captains and they went on board at 10 o'clock in a great rain.

27.9.1785

About 6 a.m. at Aqua Landing; it was a fine morning. We hear that Tom Salt[65a] or Captain Andrew's people are fighting with Combesboch's long boat. Captain Opter, the Captain of the tender, and Combesboch's Captain of the tender went down the river in the long boat to look for the boat which the Combesboch people had taken from his mate, and they got away with goods for fifteen slaves. So Tom Salt or Captain Andrew fought with the Captains and the people got the Captain out of the boat (?). One captain took thirty-two men and one woman from them and brought them back. Then all of us went to meet Duke and hear what he intends to do about it.

3.10.1785

. . . so I got together goods for Calabar Antera to go to Cameroons. Soon after that we three put our heads together and settle what we think to do and at 7 o'clock at night I put the things in Egbo Young's big canoe and at midnight I sailed to go to Curcock.

4.10.1785

About 4 o'clock I was in Egbo Young's canoe at Seven

THE DIARY OF ANTERA DUKE

Fathoms Point and saw one Egbo Sherry[66] fishing in a small canoe. So I gave him a drink of brandy and he gave me some fish. After 2 o'clock there was great rain all day until 9 o'clock.

5.10.1785

About 5 a.m. in Duke's canoe [I went] to Tom Curcock's house. I came ashore at Willy Curcock's old market place. I made my people get chop here soon after we came up. After 1 o'clock noon I went from old Curcock landing, and at the same time I saw my brother Egbo Young, Bob, and Apandam who came down all in one canoe. Then I walked up with 4 rods and one case of bottled brandy to give to Andam Curcock. Then I saw Esin.

7.10.1785

At 5 a.m. in old Curcock Town;[67] it was a fine morning so I went down to the landing and met Apandam and my brother, and saw Bob going back to Boostam. Soon afterwards I went to Enyong Creek to see Potter's mother's house but I did not find him there, so I went to Enyong town and saw one slave. Soon afterwards I found that Potter and his nice father's house had killed a goat for me; and they gave me four rods and two yards of romal.[68] Then they and the Calabar people gave me about 12 calabashes of chop in time to return that night as the creek is so bad.

10.10.1785

At about 5 a.m. in Curcock town; it was a fine morning so I went down to the landing. I gave Andam Curcock goods for one slave to live at his place. At three o'clock after noon I saw our Boostam canoe come down with five slaves and yams. At the same time I sailed away home with the slaves in my canoe and there were three small canoes besides mine.

11.10.1785

About 9 a.m. at Aqua Landing, having had no sleep; we went down to the landing and I saw Duke Sam Jack Esin

40 EFIK TRADERS OF OLD CALABAR

about Combesboch's tender. So he said it had gone away with
325 slaves. Then we got Hogan Antera and all the Ekpe men
to go with two Ekpe in a canoe to Ebrow Egbosherry's
fishermen.

23.10.1785

About 6 a.m. at Aqua Landing; it was a fine morning so we
went aboard Captain Fairweather's tender to get tea to drink.
After 11 o'clock in the morning we had one (foshin?) to blow
Ekpe on all men, ordering Egbo Young not to come and not
to go away all day before 5 o'clock. I was angry with my dear
Awa Offiong about water.[68a] Then my mother came and
'put in her word', which brought anger against my mother
so I was damn more angry about that.

24.10.1785

About 6 a.m. at Aqua Landing; a fine morning, so I went
down to the landing and I saw my canoe there. I found that
Duke had sent old Tom House to beg me to send men to catch
a cow for him. So I went myself and caught it with my own
hand. Soon afterwards Duke heard about that and he sent
me a large fish. Then I saw them taking Duke's sister's
daughter to his house to make her wear her new cloth.[69] So
all of us and Duke gave about 20 cloths and we played all
day till night. Willy Tom Robin came to play with us and I
gave him some cloth.

14.12.1785

About 5 a.m. at Aqua Landing; there was a great morning
fog; I went down to the landing to put yams in [my] canoe.
After 8 o'clock we went down in three big canoes, I, Esin, and
Egbo Young with 32 slaves. So he kept 25 slaves and about
6,000 yams. He dashed (gave) us three great guns. Some
time after 8 o'clock at night we went aboard Captain Fairweather whose tender went away with 250 slaves and two tons
[of palm-oil].

THE DIARY OF ANTERA DUKE

22.12.1785

About 6 a.m. at Aqua Landing; it was a fine morning, so we made Esin go down to [meet] Hughes. I sent two canoes with 1,500 yams for 150 coppers to pay Captain Hughes. Captain Williams went down the river carrying 169 slaves. Captain Hughes carried 480 slaves.

23.12.1785

. . . Captain Hughes went away with 484 slaves. Captain Williams went away with 160 slaves. I and Esin went on board the Cooper to break book (see note 27) for four slaves. Archibong Duke's son came home from Orroup with slaves.

25.12.1785

About 6 a.m. at Aqua Landing; a foggy morning so I went down after dressing and Captain Fairweather dressed and brought his dinner from Esin. So we all went to Esin's new house for New Year's dinner—Captain Fairweather, Tom Cooper, Captain Potter, Duke Ephraim, Coffee Duke, Egbo Young, Esin and I, Esin Ambo, Eyo Willy Honesty, and Ebitim, and we drank all day until night.

30.12.1785

About 6 a.m. at Aqua Landing and a foggy morning; I went down to the landing and found Duke there. Egbo Young went on board Captain Fairweather. I had five of my people cutting the big tree at my big cabin. At 1 o'clock after noon Tom Cooper's mate Mr. Charles came to me to nail my bed's bottom on.

31.12.1785

About 6 a.m. at Aqua Landing with a little morning fog. I went down to the landing and saw the market canoe go away and at 1 o'clock we went aboard the Cooper for dinner. After 4 o'clock we came back.

42 EFIK TRADERS OF OLD CALABAR

1.1.1786

... I saw Duke send a canoe for mimbo. After two o'clock Captain Potter brought his dinner and we had all the Captains come to chop at Esim's new house for the New Year. We saw Eyo and Ebitim go to Aqua Bakassey.

2.1.1786

About 6 a.m. at Aqua Landing; it was a fine morning so I went down to the landing and we went aboard the Cooper for tea and came ashore. At the same time I saw that Ekpe was being blown to keep anyone from coming to the house all day. After 5 o'clock we saw King Tom Salt coming to the Duke with two canoes to stay here to settle an Ekpe dispute.

3.1.1786

About 6 a.m. at Aqua Landing; a fine morning ... so Duke took a goat to make doctor (medicine) with King Tom Salt. Fairweather sent for men to come on board to get tea. Then we had chop at my house and we played at Esim's house, and took the play to Archibong's yard and played at night.

22.1.1786

At 5 a.m. at Aqua Landing with a little morning fog; I went down to the landing and sent four hands in a little canoe to take my father's Boostam mimbo to Guinea Company and to come to meet with Ephraim Offiong about war copper. At 1 o'clock Tom Cooper's tender went away with 383 slaves and 4 tons [of palm-oil].

23.1.1786

About 6 a.m. at Aqua Landing; I went down to the landing. After 8 o'clock my brother Egbo Young and Apandam came home from Boostam with the slave Toother, and we saw Tom Cooper and Captain Fairweather come up to take the tender down in Aqua [Kwa] river.

THE DIARY OF ANTERA DUKE 43

29.1.1786

At 5 a.m. at Aqua Landing; it was a fine morning so we all walked up to King Ekpe[70] to work at the palaver house. Soon afterwards we heard that King Egbo Sam Ambo had stopped three Egbosherry men at the river because they had killed one of his men. After 1 o'clock we hear that Egbo Young's dear has given birth to a young girl at Aqua town.

8.2.1786

At 5 a.m. in Aqua Bakassey Creek; it was a fine morning and I arrived at Aqua Bakassey corral at 1 o'clock. I found Archibong Duke and went alongside his canoe. I took a bottle of beer to drink with him and we called first at New Town and stayed at the landing and then went to town at 3 o'clock. We walked up to the palaver house to put the Grand Ekpe in the house and played all night. Combesboch went away with 639 slaves and Toother.[71]

11.2.1786

About 5 a.m. I was in Coqua Town and Archibong desires me to walk up to Cameroon with him, so I did and we passed 3 little Cameroon towns on the way. We walked until 1 o'clock . . . to get to Big Town. There they killed a goat and dashed me 1 iron and 2 rods. So we had a long discussion with them about Archibong's trading goods. So they paid a boy slave and begged us to drink doctor (medicine) with them. So Archibong made one of his father's sons named Ebetim drink doctor with him. They dash us one male cow to be killed and 8 rods for the chop. We came down at 6 o'clock at night.

2.3.1786

. . . Captain Potter went away with 284 slaves.

17.3.1786

. . . We came ashore and I took one goat to make doctor at my god basin. . . .

44 EFIK TRADERS OF OLD CALABAR

20.3.1786

... Soon I saw Tom Cooper coming up to say that Captain Fairweather was going away to the bar with 440 slaves. ...

21.3.1786

... Duke called all of us to come to his palaver house to hear Ephraim Egbo's daughter with him and Dick Ephraim; she says she will not marry Long Duke. We found that everything said about him was true, and we got Ephraim Duke's women to come and break Duke's god basin because he will not marry Ephraim's daughter. After 7 o'clock at night I heard that my wife Offiong's brother was dead in his father's yard and put in the ground at 6 o'clock with 8 yards of fine cloth.

20.4.1786

... I saw the people, about 200 hands, coming to me; they want me to give two of my father's sons[72] as pawns to ransom the men Eyo Duke had stopped for what they owe him; and they say one of the men is dead by Archibong Duke's hand. At the same time I saw the chief head men coming to call me out to go up into the King's palaver house to hear what they say. Soon after I saw one of my men who was left at the canoe come up and tell me that Enyong people had taken my canoe away from the landing. So I run down to the landing and find no canoe; and they take two of my boys out in the canoe and put them in irons; then they come back and stop Awa's son before my face and carry him away to put in irons. So they come down one [at a] time with about 30 hand guns, looking to shoot me; and after 2 o'clock they bring the canoe to the landing. After a long time they take the canoe back and they keep me all day without my eating anything and after 9 o'clock at night they let me have the canoe and all my men back.

1.5.1786

... So I sailed away to Aqua Bakassey and I got there at

THE DIARY OF ANTERA DUKE

1 o'clock and I called at New Town first and then went to Old Town. I fired one great gun in the creek. At the same time I found Coffee Duke here and I heard the Ekpe cry out (see p. 17) in the palaver house. So I carried 1 large case of bottled brandy and 4 rods to dash the Ekpe men and I called the town gentlemen and women and people to come and hear what I have to say. So I settled every bob and I gave Coffee 1 large case of bottled brandy and 10 yams. Coffee sailed away at 8 o'clock at night.

4.5.1786

. . . about 4 a.m. I was at Aqua Bakassey landing in Abasi Offiong's canoe. I came away from there at 10 o'clock and reached Jock Bakassey's town by 7 o'clock at night. So we carried grandy[73] to the place because they owe me goods. They paid me 1 male slave for my goods. Esim told me that they killed a cow for him and gave him 80 rods besides 16 rods for me.

18.5.1786

. . . We hear that John Cobham's family are making a play for their father, so they cut 7 men's heads off (see note 60).

21.5.1786

I sent 10 hands to work in the bush. After 10 o'clock we got the Bush Ekpe to stop all men from coming up and I had Esim and John Cooper to chop (eat) at my house. Tom Cooper went away with 381 slaves.

10.6.1786

We had Duke send all the Ekpe men to go to King Ekpe to share some copper [rods] that Tom Salt brought for the little Ekpe palaver. So the Ekpe men take 40 coppers to send Egbosherry away and one goat is killed for them. At 3 o'clock we saw two new ships coming up, Captain Ford and one French ship, so we went on board the two and then ashore to Duke.

46 EFIK TRADERS OF OLD CALABAR

23.6.1786

Duke sent a boy to come and call we three, so we went and found Eyo Willy Honesty here with the French comey book. So Duke told we three to go on board with Eyo; so we got aboard the ship and went down to look at the book. We found that all the Henshaw Town [people] had taken comey more than what they got for every ship.[74] We came ashore and had chop at Abasi's.

2.7.1786

About 5 a.m. at Aqua Landing, and a fine morning. I went to see Duke who was a little sick. At 8 o'clock at night we all took two goats to go and 'make doctor' with Duke.

3.7.1786

About 5 a.m. at Aqua Landing and a fine morning. I went to see Duke, who is sick. After 1 o'clock we all went to Duke's yard to eat the goats we used to make doctor and at 7 o'clock at night Duke was very bad.

4.7.1786

About 4 o'clock in the morning Duke Ephraim died. Soon after we came up to look where to put him in the ground.[75]

5.7.1786

About 5 o'clock we put Duke in the ground. Nine men and women went with him, and we all looked very poor. Captain Savage arrived.

6.7.1786

... we went on board every ship in five canoes to let all the Captains know.

9.7.1786

... after 10 o'clock at night I had Esim, Egbo Young, and Coffee Duke come to my house to look at Duke's comey book and think what should be done.

THE DIARY OF ANTERA DUKE 47

10.7.1786

... All the Cobham Town gentlemen met at George Cobham's yard with our family to chop doctor with us, and return.[76] At 9 o'clock we walked up to Long Dick's cabin with our gentlemen to drink our family doctor.

11.7.1786

... at 9 o'clock at night we chop doctor with the Henshaw Family at Long Dick's cabin.

18.7.1786

... at 3 o'clock after noon King Aqua came down with 157 men and 16 women and girls; we told him to walk up to George Cobham's, then we and all the Calabar gentlemen went to meet here and drink doctor with Aqua.

19.7.1786

... our family met with Long Tom who is King Aqua, to drink doctor with him, and at 7 o'clock at night our family met Willy Tom Robin to drink doctor with him.

9.8.1786

... Esim told me that a Bakassey gentleman who feared to come here when Duke was alive has now come, and we put our heads together to carry him on board ship to put him in irons, and also two of his slaves. I carried him on board myself.

4.9.1786

... about 6 a.m. at Aqua Landing with a fine morning. We saw a Frenchman drop down. So Esim and I went down with 2 cows (canoes?) and came back after 3 o'clock. We saw six Captains putting their heads together; they said that the Frenchman had taken a mate belonging to the Brighouse[77] tender and one of John Cooper's white men, and three men belonging to Savage, on board the Frenchman; they said that eight men in all were aboard the Frenchman. So all the

EFIK TRADERS OF OLD CALABAR

Captains went on board the Savage and got everything ready. Then we saw Eyo and Ebetim coming to tell us and see about that, and we all went down in our eight canoes, to beg the French Captain to let us have the white men back. He would not let us have the men. At the same time we saw them take Savage's ship and come down. So they said there must be a fight to get those white men. So we came up and left those two ships there. At 11 o'clock at night Eyo and Ebetim drank tea in young Duke's new house. We stayed there a little time and then Eyo and Ebetim went to their town to let Willy Honesty hear that news.

5.10.1786

... I saw that Coffee Duke sent his son to tell me news about a new ship. After a little time I heard 5 great guns fired at Seven Fathoms Point and we saw the ship come up. It was John Cooper's tender arriving, so we fired three great guns for him.

9.10.1786

... we heard great firing in Aqua River and after 4 o'clock we saw one tender come up. It was Captain Johnston's ship with the tender of Captain Aspinal. So we fired three great guns.

10.10.1786

I went to my back cabin to plant some mimbo trees and all our family walked up to the new palaver house and took one young boy slave to make doctor,[78] and two guns to be fired for the doctor; one gun fired and broke Long Dick Ephraim's hand. Dick must lose one of his hands by that gun.

14.10.1786

... after 10 o'clock I walked up to the new palaver house to work and at 7 o'clock at night Egbosherry sent word to let us know that Egbosherry Sam Ambo had caught seven men. They were coming by water in 20 canoes. So we sent the

THE DIARY OF ANTERA DUKE

Ekpe drum to blow, forbidding everyone in the town to come
or go to market. I sent one good canoe to go up Curcock
River to take care of my cabin boy.

15.10.1786

... I was thinking all day about my cabin boy who had gone
to Curcock for fear he should be caught and I could not eat
all day. At 7 o'clock I found he had come home.

19.10.1786

... I played Aqua doctor with one Aqua man. So I killed
one goat for my god, and had dinner with Captain Aspinal
and the Captain of his tender in my house. Eyo Willy Honesty
sent my brother Egbo Young to Esim Duke about some
Curcock dispute.

26.10.1786

... I put water in my belly.[79] Then I heard that Ekpe was
run and when I heard I walked up to Egbo Young. We saw
Ekpe come down and the Ekpe men said that Sam Ambo
and George Cobham had blown [Ekpe] on Captain Fairweather (see note 36). So all our family were damn angry
about that blow and we sent to call Captain Fairweather to
come ashore and break trade first with our family for about 15
slaves and we fired three guns on shore. At 3 o'clock in the
afternoon we saw Eyo and Ebetim come down with Esin
Ambo, and they went to Sam and George Cobham to make
them settle with Captain Fairweather.

2.11.1786

About 5 a.m. at Aqua Landing; it was a fine morning and
all our family went to Creek Town to make a play. First
Creek Town cut one woman slave's head off, and one cow was
killed and a goat, and we fired seven great guns. We came
back at 5 o'clock. After 9 o'clock at night Esim Duke came to
my cabin to break one puncheon of brandy and share it with
all Duke's [family] and sisters. So we had our canoe (?) go

EFIK TRADERS OF OLD CALABAR

up to Guinea Company with Apandam to fetch wood and palaver house drink.

4.11.1786

I went on board Captain Fairweather and saw Efi(om) come up with 3 canoes and play Ekpe in them. After they came up to the landing with Ekpe all the men and women were crying in the town for Duke (see p. 23). I sent my people for wood in two canoes.

6.11.1786

About 4 a.m. I got up; there was great rain, so I walked to the town palaver house and I found all the gentlemen here. So we got ready to cut heads off and at 5 o'clock in the morning we began to cut slaves' heads off, fifty heads off in that one day. I carried 29 cases of bottled brandy, and 15 calabashes of chop for everybody, and there was play in every yard in town.

7.11.1786

About 4 a.m. at Aqua Landing and a fine morning. So I made all the women bring calabashes to make chop to give to everybody, and all the people played all day and all night. All the gentlemen went to dinner at Esim Duke's.

8.11.1786

. . . I saw Jack Bakassey come and bring one woman slave to be beheaded in honour of my father, and I sent my Yellow Hogan Abasi to market.[80] All the gentlemen had dinner at Egbo Young's. We heard news about a new ship. Three more heads were cut off.

9.11.1786

. . . about 4 a.m. at Aqua Landing. I made all the women bring calabashes to make chop. Soon after one Taeon town [man] cut off the head of a Backsider town [man], and brought it here for his Duke play. I have all the gentlemen to dinner with me.

THE DIARY OF ANTERA DUKE 51

10.11.1786

. . . after 8 o'clock we made the Bush Ekpe men blow everybody to stay inside their houses[81] . . . by 4 o'clock all were playing again and played all night.

11.11.1786

About 4 o'clock we went into the town palaver house and we [were] dressed [to go to] the town again in long cloth and Ekpe cloth[82] and hat and jacket and many fine things. Obong Ekpe ran in town till at 1 o'clock we finished that.

12.11.1786

. . . I made all the women bring calabashes to make chop. Grandy (see note 73) Ekpe was again taken to the women and there were plays all day and night.

13.11.1786

About 5 a.m. at Aqua Landing with a fine morning. I went down to the landing to look for a place to make a dwelling house. Soon after that all the Ekpe men made all the Duke women pay 55 coppers to Ekpe.[83] After 8 o'clock at night all the Ekpe people met in the palaver house and made all Duke's wives come and cry the Ekpe cry in the town palaver house (see p. 17).

8.12.1786

. . . I went down to the landing to get all the guns ready and we fired 28 great guns ashore, one for each ship. We had shaved our heads first,[84] and we wore fine hats and fine clothes and handkerchiefs. All the Captains and we gentlemen had dinner at Esim's house.

9.12.1786

About 6 a.m. at Aqua Landing; there was a small morning fog. I walked up to see an Egbosherry play.[85] We wore new cloth. At midnight Captain Fairweather's tender went away with 280 slaves.

E

52 EFIK TRADERS OF OLD CALABAR

19.12.1786

... I walked up to Esim and Egbo Young; Esim was playing
with some country people living near Guinea Company side.
They had come to see us about Duke's death. After that we
went on board ship. After midnight Captain Brighouse's
tender went away with 420 slaves.

24.12.1786

... we had Ekpe running about town and after 7 o'clock at
night we read a letter which had come to Willy Honesty about
what Ekpe money they would put for Willy and Tom Curcock:
40 men first and 13 men more for the Cobham family. In
Aqua landing that. . . .

25.12.1786

About 5 a.m. at Aqua Landing. I dressed, and Esim and
Egbo Young. So Esim and Egbo Young's canoe went to
Boostam and after 1 o'clock in the afternoon all the Captains
dressed and came ashore to dinner at Esim Duke's house with
us gentlemen and Willy Tom Robin.

28.12.1786

... so all our family came to meet Young Tom Curcock
about his saying that Duke owed his father 2 boxes of rods
and three slaves. So all our family found that this was a damn
lie.

1.1.1787

About 5 a.m. at Aqua Landing; there was a small morning
fog. I made 8 calabashes of Ekpe chop and at one o'clock we
and all the Captains had dinner at Egbo Young's house, Liverpool Hall. At 3 o'clock we put money for 17 men to be Calabar
Ekpe.

24.1.1787

... so I saw that Egbo Young had sent one of his men to
come and call me. So all the Duke family walked up to Egbo

THE DIARY OF ANTERA DUKE 53

Young's house and had a great dispute about Ekpe. I and Ephraim Aqua said some angry words to him; I because of some words he had spoken about my father. Willy Tom Robin has paid more Ekpe money, Long Duke more Ekpe money belonging to Imo Duke's son. Willy Honesty and the Cobham family gave Old Town Ekpe money for 41 men.

31.1.1787

... so I walked up to Esim and Egbo Young after we heard that Aqua Bakassey was in the river. I and Egbo Young went down to the landing to see, and at 12 o'clock we saw Old Town coming, so we went down to fetch them up and saw them put money for 51 men, Henshaw town put for 8 men, Willy Tom for one. 60 men in all they caught for us and at 7 o'clock at night they went home.

1.2.1787

... at 7 o'clock at night Captain Aspinal's tender went away with 300 slaves.

2.2.1787

... Willy Honesty was playing Ekpe and came to my yard, so I gave him 1 piece of India Roosnall,[86] 1 gin stuff, 1 rod for his play people, and one case of French bottled brandy, 1 long white bottle of brandy. After that we all walked up to his house to meet about first war copper. (?)

16.2.1787

... Egbo Young and Willy Honesty dressed Grandy Ekpe in the palaver house. So we bought Ekpe 344 men to be the Calabar new Ekpe.

17.2.1787

... at 6 o'clock at night we found that Long Dick had some Ekpe palaver with a Boostam man. So all the old Ekpe were damn angry and blew all the new Ekpe [so that they should not] sleep at the Ekpe palaver house.

54 EFIK TRADERS OF OLD CALABAR

20.2.1787

At the same time we saw that Willy Tom Robin had sent one of his boys to tell us that one of my dear father's sons named Ebo was dead from a two day sickness. So I made my dear Awa Offiong go with 6 of my men to 'make grandy'. At 7 o'clock at night my dear came back.

22.2.1787

. . . about 5 a.m. at Aqua Landing, with some morning fog. So we walked up to see Willy Honesty. All the old Ekpe and I and Esim met at the Ekpe palaver house to decide who is to be Old Calabar Ekpe. All the Ekpe men decide that Ephraim Aqua's son is not the town Ekpe, and [neither is] Robin Henshaw's son nor Henshaw Robin Henshaw. So all the old and new Ekpe blew for them not to be Ekpe men and after 8 o'clock at night I and Esim carried one jug, 2 long cases of white bottled brandy, 1 large jar of mimbo up to the Ekpe house to give to all the old and new Ekpe to drink, and came back at 2 o'clock at night.

26.2.1787

. . . at 8 o'clock at night Long King Aqua sent one of his gentlemen to be killed by our hands so we sent that gentleman by Long Duke to the river to be killed.[87]

3.3.1787

About 5 we went on board Captain Fairweather to take comey for Ephraim Aqua and Ephraim, and Coffee and Archibong, and we came ashore with all the Captains. Then every ship fired guns. One gun came up and cut one of Captain Tatam's white men's head off.

17.3.1787

. . . so Eyo and Ebetim and Esin came with Ekpe to Hogan about the business of a poor boy for Ekpe. So all made him pay 335 coppers and give one house-boy to Ekpe for his head to be cut off.[88] Soon after they came home again.

THE DIARY OF ANTERA DUKE

24.3.1787

. . . at 12 o'clock Willy Honesty called all the gentlemen to meet in Egbo Cobham's cabin to decide who we will make King of Old Calabar, and after 7 o'clock at night all of us town gentlemen met at Coffee's cabin to settle every bad quarrel we had had since our father died. So we killed 2 goats.

13.4.1787

. . . we had chop in Egbo Young's house. We saw all the Henshaw family coming to ask our family to let them know who we will make King Ekpe. So we said we don't know as we first must settle about the King of Calabar.[89]

16.4.1787

. . . we went to Creek Town in 2 good canoes and one small one to meet (?) the Guinea Company and Old Town about the two towns wanting to pay Ekpe in one day. So we said we had never heard that since our great-grandfather's time. So Willy killed a goat for us and I walked to Henshaw town to see my mimbo wife[90] and came home at 2 o'clock after noon.

18.4.1787

. . . Otto Ephraim and Willy Tom Robin came to ask us if we will pay them first or the Guinea Company first. We say we will pay them first; I have sent my cabin [boy] to the mimbo market.

28.4.1787

About 5 a.m. I was lying in bed. I saw Coffee Duke come to me and make my cabin boy call me to him. So he told me about a manatee being killed in King Aqua landing. So I made 7 hands go with Jimmy Antera to fetch it into Aqua river.[91] So we drank all day to my girl-wife in Duke's sister's daughter's house.

30.4.1787

. . . I made my Hogan Abasi go to my father's mimbo

EFIK TRADERS OF OLD CALABAR

place to fetch mimbo. After 10 o'clock in the day we blew [Ekpe] to stop men from coming up, because we were going to eat Bush Ekpe chop in the palaver house. I walked with the Ekpe drum to the landing; at the same time we saw that Ephraim Watt was not afraid to come with seven of his men. So we walked back into the palaver house, and all the Bush Ekpe men sent word [to Ephraim Watt] to pay seven goats; so he sent coppers for six goats and one goat for that palaver.

21.5.1787

About 6 a.m. at Aqua Landing with a fine morning. We saw that Captain Ford had sent his tender away last night with 330 slaves. We settled comey on board the Potter and we came ashore at 4 o'clock.

26.5.1787

... I hear that 18 male slaves took a boat and ran away from John Cooper last night and at 5 o'clock after noon we hear that some of those slaves are at Aqua Town.

27.5.1787

... All Captain John's family came to see us about one of their daughters who married Egbo Young and had fought with another wife and broken her teeth out. So they came to break the other wife's teeth out. We made Jimmy Antera take out the teeth of the wife, the daughter of Ephraim Robin Henshaw.

4.6.1787

... 7 o'clock at night we hear that Captain Aspinal is dead and hear all the town cry out. Ndem Ephraim has married Long Duke (see p. 44).

5.6.1787

... all the Captains came ashore to bury Captain Aspinal with much ceremony. So we fired 6 great guns ashore.

THE DIARY OF ANTERA DUKE 57

7.6.1787

. . . we saw Robin Tom, King John and Otto Ditto Tom; King John sent them to come and make a play in honour of Duke and my father, and Egbo Young's mother; so they cut one woman's head off for Duke and seven Bar Room men were to be beheaded for my father. So they played all night.

11.6.1787

. . . at 3 o'clock after noon Captain Hewitt and Combesboch and one little ship belonging to Hewitt came for 60 slaves, and Aspinal's mate lost both hands by the firing of guns.

15.6.1787

. . . John Cooper dashed Esim and Egbo Young 2 great guns, and we came ashore. We hear that King Aqua has made all his wives drink doctor. So 11 wives died from drinking doctor (see p. 22). John Cooper dropped down river about 8 o'clock at night.

16.7.1787

. . . Captain Aspinal's ship goes away with 328 slaves.

18.7.1787

. . . Sam Ambo began to cut (sacrifice) a cow for his god to make a play. Eyo and Ebetim and Esien sent word to let us know that they were coming to see Sam King Ambo cut his cow.

25.7.1787

. . . I went to make a play in King Ambo's yard about his cutting the cow for his god and I saw Eyo Willy Honesty come at the same time. At 11 o'clock at night I came back with the members of my play.

26.7.1787

. . . at 3 o'clock we went to Cobham Town where every man

58 EFIK TRADERS OF OLD CALABAR

again gave Sam King Ambo coppers for the cutting of the cow for his god. So he got 986 coppers from all Calabar. At the same time it rained hard, and we came back; it rained all night.

1.8.1787

. . . I went up to my work place and went into the Ekpe palaver house and I found that somebody had stolen the door from the Ekpe palaver house. So we sent the drum to make all our new Ekpe men come to the palaver house, and we send about 3 Ekpe to every yard to see if they will find it.

11.8.1787

. . . after 2 o'clock all the Captains and the Calabar gentlemen met at King Ambo's palaver house to talk about a fight between one of Willy Curcock's men and Captain Ford's mate. Soon after the mate died, so we decided that Willy Curcock's man should have his ear cut off because of the fight.

13.8.1787

. . . we hear that Captain Brighouse went away with 320 slaves.

14.8.1787

. . . we hear that John Tom Henshaw is dead. So we sent our people to Henshaw Town with Apandam.

18.8.1787

. . . I had Captain Potter come ashore; after 11 o'clock Potter sent his tender and his ship to bring 35 white men and at noon they began to put up two sides of the house; and after 2 p.m. I have all the Captains to dinner and supper with me.

25.8.1787

. . . at 4 o'clock after noon Captain Fairweather's tender went away with 210 slaves. . . .

THE DIARY OF ANTERA DUKE

31.8.1787

... I heard that John Tom Cobham's wife hanged herself about the palaver of October 17th, 1787.[92] Jimmy Henshaw paid his [assessment] for 4 Calabar afaws[93] to be King Ekpe.

Willy Honesty	.	20 rods and one goat
George Old Town	.	10 rods
Tom Nonaw	.	10 rods
Old and New Ekpe	.	8 rods
Robin Curcock	.	5 rods
Guinea Company	.	
King Ekpe	.	5 rods
Eyamba	.	10 rods
Old and New Ekpe		8 rods
Tom Cobham	.	10 rods
Duke Ephraim	.	20 rods and goat
Egbo Young Offiong		25 rods and one goat
Robin John	.	5 rods
John Ambo	.	5 rods
Willy Tom	.	4 rods
Tom Curcock	.	5 rods
Old and New Ekpe	.	8 rods
Effar	.	5 rods
Misimbo	.	4 rods
King Ambo	.	20 rods and goat
Ephraim Aqua	.	5 rods

5.9.1787

... we carried Ekpe into King Ambo's [place] because one of Tatam's pawns had run away. So we made him give one of his sons to Tatam.

16.9.1787

... we carried Grand Ekpe to Henshaw and Willy Tom to blow forbidding any Captain to send any Calabar pawn,

EFIK TRADERS OF OLD CALABAR

which was given for my slave goods, away in his tender. Tatam's tender went away with 330 slaves.

19.9.1787

... after 12 o'clock noon we had dinner in my house and drank fine mimbo. We heard one gun fired so we made two or three boys run to find out who was firing guns. They came back and told us that my Yellow Hogan Abasi had shot his wife with a gun but the shot did not hit her.

20.9.1787

... My Yellow Hogan Abasi's wife named Eba came to me and she said she had eaten 'doctor' and I sent for my dear. So my dear sends word that she vomits, so I tell my dear to carry her to my mother to give her more doctor to drink. Afterwards I went on board. Then my mother sent word to me saying the wife of my Yellow Hogan is dead. Soon we hear that one little snow (?) British ship was in the Cameroons to get sail. I had the carpenter begin to lay the floor of my new house.

Here is written in	Antera Duke Ejus Liber
another hand	Archibald Forrest Thomas Taylor

26.9.1787

About 6 a.m. at Aqua Landing, with a fine morning. This day there were nine ships in the river. Willy Honesty and all of us went on board the snow British ship to settle comey palaver. He will pay 1000 coppers for every Calabar. Old Otto Duke's daughter drank doctor with her husband's wife.

1.10.1787

... I saw two of King Aqua's women slaves coming from my yard. They broke one of my god basins,[94] and said they would be [my] slaves. So I sent word to King Aqua to let him know, and after 2 o'clock we all four new and old Calabar Ekpe went to meet at King Ambo's palaver house about Willy Curcock's Ekpe palaver.

THE DIARY OF ANTERA DUKE 61

3.10.1787

... this day there were 10 ships in the river. I sent my cabin boy Eyo Ebrow's son to the mimbo market. Soon after we heard of a new ship in Parrot Island.

9.10.1787

... Willy Honesty sent to us to come on board the Rogers for a meeting. So we collected 500 coppers to give Robin John for his comey and to have it named in the comey book.

17.10.1787

... I walked up to Egbo Young and Esim, and afterwards we came down to my house and sent my cabin boy to Apandam's cabin to fetch 115 [coppers] belonging to Jimmy. Then we began to share out among all four Calabar Ekpe to make Jimmy Henshaw King Ekpe.

22.10.1787

... we heard that all the Creek Town gentlemen had come with Willy Honesty to King Ambo's place; so we and all the men and women went to King Ambo's palaver house. Then Willy sent on board Captain Fairweather to call Coffee Duke, and he came ashore with Captain Fairweather. So the Calabar [people] began to ask him what made him run away on board. After these words he says he heard that we four had drunk doctor to kill him. So we told the Calabar that we had drunk doctor [and sworn] that not one of us would go to his house because we heard Duke's sister say that he had killed Duke; [we said] let him drink doctor with Duke's sister before we settle; at the same time we sent to call Duke's sister, and she came to the palaver house. Afterwards she began to bring the dispute to all the Calabar ... and she says she wants to drink doctor with Coffee. So everybody asks Coffee to drink doctor with her, but Coffee would not drink doctor. So we tell Willy Honesty to send two Ekpe drums to carry Coffee to his house, and we say we four will not settle with Coffee if he does not drink doctor.

62 EFIK TRADERS OF OLD CALABAR

25.10.1787

About 6 a.m. at Aqua Landing; there was a little rain, so I walked up to see Esim and Egbo Young. I saw Jimmy Henshaw coming to see us and we told him to go on board the Rogers to take comey for all the Henshaw family, and we went on board the Rogers to have Jimmy Henshaw's name as King Ekpe put in the comey book. I heard that all the Captains were meeting on board Captain Ford about Hogan Captain Duke's fight with Ford. Soon after 2 o'clock we came ashore and I heard that one of my Ephraim Abasi's Egbosherry women has borne two sons in one day. . . .[95] Ndem Duke's wife bore a young girl in Aqua town.

1.11.1787

. . . at 12 o'clock midday we went on board Captain Fairweather for dinner. Soon afterwards we went on board every ship to let them know that I am going to Aqua Bakassey to buy canoes, and after midnight I sailed away from the landing to go to Aqua Bakassey. I took two of Esim Duke's girls with me, and one girl belonging to my dear, that makes 3 girls. We were 42 hands besides the 3 girls in two canoes.

2.12.1787

. . . we found that Captain Fairweather's doctor was dead, and we saw Ekpe run about the town.

4.12.1787

. . . I had my girl, Archibong Duke's son's sister, put large copper leg manacles on her leg,[96] and I paid the smith one rod, 5 Boostam yams, and one jar of mimbo.

11.12.1787

. . . Tom John Cobham's dear wife drank doctor, all must die. I made my dear go to Henshaw Town to see him because she is his sister, and Esim's dear went to see him. At 9 o'clock at night my dear came back. Ndem Nothing[97] came home from Orroup.

THE DIARY OF ANTERA DUKE

13.12.1787

. . . we sent Esim to go and see John Cobham in Henshaw Town and at 5 o'clock we 3 brothers walked up to Henshaw Town to Jimmy Henshaw's yard. So Jimmy killed a goat for us, and we went into his cabin and stayed there and called all the gentlemen for a long discussion and came back at 9 o'clock.

22.12.1787

. . . Potter and his tender went away with 350 slaves.

25.12.1787

. . . great morning fog, and at 1 o'clock we had Captain Fairweather, John Tatam, Captain Ford, Captain Hughes, Captain Potter, Captain Rogers and Captain Combesboch and Eyo Willy Honesty, and Willy Tom Robin. We had dinner in Duke's house and supper. At 8 o'clock at night they went on board, and we fired three guns.

29.12.1787

. . . at 3 o'clock after noon Captain Fairweather went away with 377 slaves.

1.1.1788

About 5 a.m. at Aqua Landing with a great fog. I went down to the landing. I made my girl, Archibong Duke's son's sister, wear a cloth for the first time, and be a woman. At 1 o'clock we had dinner with six Captains in Egbo Young's house.

3.1.1788

. . . I went on board to get some brandy for two of my brothers, and at 3 o'clock after noon my two brothers and my Ephraim Abasi went away from Orroup. At the same time we heard that Captain John King Ekpe had died in the Old Town palaver house in front of all the gentlemen.

64 EFIK TRADERS OF OLD CALABAR

7.1.1788

... Robin John sent one of his old men to come and say that everybody is wanted to go and take doctor to see if he killed Captain John King Ekpe or not.

8.1.1788

... One of Willy Honesty's men came and told me that Coffee Duke has said he will come here and set fire to all his houses. So I took 2 Ekpe drums and blew to forbid any men to sleep in the houses. At the same time I heard that Ndem Duke's son had died from a bad sickness.[98]

9.1.1788

... old Robin John came himself and called the Calabar gentlemen to go to King Ambo's palaver house and meet, because they say that Robin John killed Captain John Ambo. So everyone agreed that it was not true. Duke came home from Orroup.

17.1.1788

... about 6 a.m. at Aqua Landing with a fine morning. I went on board the Ford and came back at 10 o'clock and drank in my house. At 6 o'clock I blew all ... Ekpe men to cut firewood again in the morning to put in the town palaver house. After 9 o'clock at night I saw that fire had got into Potter Antera's yard. So I went up on top of the house myself, and every man, to catch the fire. The fire had caught four houses. Soon afterwards I saw Willy Tom Robin come and Captain Tatam sent one mate and six boat boys to help me.

23.1.1788

... I went on board to see Captain Potter about his cooper who was drowned in the water last night about 8 o'clock. We saw the Combesboch tender go away with 280 slaves. At 2 o'clock after noon King Aqua came to see Egbo Young Offiong, so we played all afternoon; at 7 o'clock at night he went home, and soon after we carried Grand Ekpe into the palaver house.

THE DIARY OF ANTERA DUKE 65

27.1.1788

About 5 a.m. at Aqua Landing with a great morning fog. So I walked up to see the carpenters and joiners. After that Backsider Drek Cameroons came to us with the new Obong men, so I gave them four rods. We went aboard the Ford for dinner.

31.1.1788

About 5 a.m. at Aqua Landing with a great morning fog. So I went down to the landing and I sent my son on board the Hughes to call him ashore and give him slaves, and after that I and Egbo Young and Esin Duke went on board the Rogers. At 1 o'clock noon I sent two of my father's sons to the mimbo market.

NOTES ON THE DIARY OF ANTERA DUKE

D. Simmons

1. The name Antera is probably *Ntiero* in Efik, and is peculiar to the Duke family of Duke Town. Besides the author of this diary, Waddell (1863, pp. 337, 498) mentions an Antera Duke, while an Efik gentleman named Ntiero Efiom Duke now lives in Calabar.

1a. Aqua is probably the diarist's transcription of the Efik adjective *akwa*, 'big', rather than a reference to the neighbouring village, Big Qua Town, whose inhabitants are culturally related to the Ejagham Ekoi, and are called *abakpa* by the Efik. The 'big landing' was presumably situated somewhere along the present Marina of Duke Town.

2. The Efik word *ekpe*, 'leopard', is substituted for the diarist's word 'egbo' even though 'egbo' is sanctioned by continual usage among Europeans since the nineteenth century. Egbo, more properly *ekpo* since Efik lacks the voiced labial velar *gb*, might be confused with the Ibibio masked society known as *ekpo*, 'ghost', which does not exist among the Efik.

3. The word 'dash' is of dubious origin, although used extensively in West Africa to denote any gift or present. Winwood Reade (1863, p. 22) opines that the word derives from the Portuguese *das-me*, 'give me'. The present commentator suggests that the derivation is from the English phrase 'dash of rum', which was frequently given to natives when they came aboard ships to trade. The *O.E.D.* derives the word from an alleged native word *dashee* and gives the first date of its occurrence as 1723. The word occurs in German as early as 1603 (De Bry, p. 29) under the form, *dache*.

4. The Efik formerly had a currency of copper and iron rods and copper wire; see p. 5.

NOTES ON THE DIARY 67

5. A plot of land belonging to the Ekpe Society; see p. 17.

6. A 'bob' signifies a dispute or quarrel. Hutchinson (1861, p. 19) remarks that the term 'bob' has a meaning in some degree resembling that signified by 'palaver', and seems to be an abbreviation of the slang word, 'bobbery'. There is a trade 'bob' and a war 'bob', as well as a hate 'bob' and a respect 'bob'.

7. Egbo Young is an anglicization of *Ekpenyɔŋ*, the name of a supernatural power, as well as a personal name. Persons so named are believed to be self-willed and unruly, since the actions of the *Ekpenyɔŋ* supernatural power are unpredictable.

8. Otto is an anglicization of the Efik name *Otu*.

9. The word 'palaver' derives from the Portuguese *palavra* or Spanish *palabra*, 'word', and signifies any discussion, debate, or conference. The word is so intimately associated with the West African coast that Francis Grosse in his *Classical Dictionary* (1785) erroneously imputes to it an African origin.

10. The judges evidently decided against Egbo Young, since he contributed a goat as well as court costs. Both plaintiff and defendant pay equal fees to have a case adjudicated. The loser gives a goat to provide a feast for everyone and thus signifies that he accepts the judgement, bears no ill-will to his opponent or the judges, and will comply with the decision.

11. Duke is an anglicization of the Efik name *Orok*.

12. This passage refers to the number of fees received from new initiates to the Ekpe Society.

13. Slaves were obtained by 'trust-trade'; see p. 4.

14. Eyo Willy Honesty is the renowned Efik warrior-chieftain Eyo Nsa of Creek Town, who died in 1820, according to the editors of Crow (1836, p. 280). Eyo Nsa obtained his European name through scrupulous fairness in his trading with Europeans. He is reputed to have decapitated the chiefs of Old Town, Enyong, and Itu through various stratagems. There may be some substance in the claim, for Eyo Nsa decapitated the chief of Old Town during the sudden war in 1767 between Duke Town and Old Town, when the Duke

68 EFIK TRADERS OF OLD CALABAR

Town warriors, with the connivance of some European ships' captains, suddenly attacked the Old Town warriors during a peace parley aboard European ships. George Millar (*Abridgement*, III, pp. 155-6) testified that he saw Willy Honesty decapitate an important Old Town man after obtaining the man from the custody of an English ship's captain by saying, 'Captain, if you will give me that man to cut cutty head, I will give you the best man in my canoe and you shall be slaved the first ship.'

15. The compound of a chief consisted of several rectangular rooms and courtyards surrounded by a high wall of wattle and daub; the sloping roofs were composed of rectangular thatch mats attached to a framework of poles. Slaves and loyal retainers inhabited the outermost courtyard to protect the chief in case of any surreptitious assault on the compound. The chief lived in one of the inner courtyards, another being used by his wives.

16. Efik hospitality requires the provision of food for visitors, as recorded incidents throughout the diary illustrate. A host who does not offer food and drink insults his guest.

17. Duke Town is situated on slightly rising terrain immediately surrounded by a steep hillside. Possibly the diarist walked up the hill towards Henshaw Town to admire the panorama of Duke Town.

18. The Efik fortified the beach with cannon and also fired cannon at funeral obsequies or to salute the arrival of European ships. Various types of cannon are still to be found in many Efik compounds.

19. Henshaw Town, or *Nsiduŋ*, is one mile south of Duke Town.

20. Presumably Honesty's daughter celebrated the wearing of her first cloth which required her family, relatives, and friends to mark her newly acquired status by giving her gifts (see p. 15).

21. The Efik verb root *bre*, 'play', signifies all types of singing, music, or dancing, whether performed by an individual or a group.

NOTES ON THE DIARY

22. Possibly this is Captain Smale, who commanded the *Hawke* of Liverpool in 1780 (see Williams, 1897, p. 280). Ships are usually referred to in the diary by the name of their Captains.

23. The Efik purchased slaves from neighbouring towns with which they had established trade relations, but also went on war expeditions to capture slaves from other villages (see p. 7).

24. All members of the Leopard (Ekpe) Society receive a share of the initiation fees received from new members.

25. Important chiefs possessed two-storey wooden houses (see p. 8).

26. Boostam is believed to be Mbiabo, a town on the right bank of the Cross River above Ikot Offiong.

27. 'Break book' signifies the establishment of a trading agreement and derives from the European trader opening his account book to enter the transaction.

28. Esin is the Duke Town pronunciation of a name pronounced *Esien* in Creek Town, and is one of the few examples of variant pronunciation in Efik.

29. With regard to Parrot Island, Hutchinson (1858, p. 112) relates: 'A curious superstition is connected with Parrot Island, and is observed with religious punctuality by the natives of Old Kalabar, on the occasion of need arising for its performance. Whenever a scarcity of European trading ships exists, or is apprehended, the Duketown authorities are accustomed to take an Albino child of their own race, and offer it up as a sacrifice at Parrot Island, to the God of the white man. This they do because the island is in view of the sea . . . over which the God of the nations that sent them articles of European manufacture is supposed to preside. The last sacrifice of this kind was made within the past year. . . .'

30. Cobham Town is probably the small Efut community south-east of Duke Town. Cobham is an anglicization of the Efik name, *Akabom*.

70   EFIK TRADERS OF OLD CALABAR

31. Guinea Company is the English name for the Efik town of Adiabo, situated on the west bank of the Calabar River approximately ten miles from Duke Town.

32. The Duke is annoyed as he loses the customs fees which he would have received if the ship had remained to trade at Duke Town (see p. 6).

33. The Duke's wife either saved his life by preventing an explosion of gunpowder or threatened to blow him up with gunpowder. The latter is rather unlikely. The Efik were often careless in storing gunpowder. Waddell (1863, p. 289) records an explosion in the Duke Town market in 1846 which killed several and injured many more.

34. Ephraim is an anglicization of the Efik name, *Efiom*.

35. Canoes frequently capsize on the Calabar River. Efik believe that a supernatural female power called *Udominyaŋ*, also known as *mami wɔta*, 'mother water' in pidgin English, seizes the goods which fall into the river. Any canoe which carries any type of ceremonial play or a corpse always has the new leaves of the oil-palm tree hanging from the bow to prevent any supernatural power capsizing it.

36. The editors of Crow's *Memoirs* (1830, pp. 282-3) note that ' "to blow Egbo" upon anyone who is a European . . . in cases of disagreement between the chiefs and the captains . . . causes a suspension of intercourse until the parties come to an understanding'. This may also apply between Efik, as the instance reveals. Since the youth flouted the authority of the Society, the members seized a goat from his mother as punishment. Had the boy not been the son of the chief, the punishment would undoubtedly have been greater.

37. Orroup is the Ododop tribe who inhabit the southern Cameroons. The Okoyong, who live north of the Efik, evidently migrated from the Ododop tribe. According to Goldie (1874, pp. 353-61), Ododop '. . . is reached by way of the Qua River and in going to it from Calabar, two days are spent travelling on the river, and one on land, when the village Ekonganaku is reached. . . .'

38. Curcock is the Efik town, Ikot Offiong, also known as

NOTES ON THE DIARY

Tom Ekrikok's town. Curcock presumably derives from the name *Ekrikɔk*.

39. Mimbo is the juice obtained by tapping the wine-palm tree. The Efik word for palm-wine is *mmin efik*, 'Efik wine'. Fresh palm-wine is non-alcoholic, but approximately six hours after being tapped it begins to ferment.

40. 'Make doctor' is a pidgin-English term denoting any type of sacrifice, oath-swearing, or any form of 'medicine'.

41. The words 'god basin' appear to be a direct translation of *usan abasi*, 'basin of god'. Waddell (1863, p. 381) states: 'A little tree of a particular kind grew in every man's yard . . . At the foot of it were one or two earthen pans, or basins, containing a little water. Beside it were generally seen human skulls, and over it a land-turtle hanging to the tree. The water in the basins was never emptied out, but every prayer-day a little more was added, and something like a prayer or wish expressed for safety, success, and length of life. The basin was called God's dish. It was said that they called on their fathers on these occasions. Sometimes prayer was made over goats and fowls killed for friends arriving and leaving. . . .' He also reports (p. 398) that the basins were discarded in 1849 at the behest of King Eyo II, a son of the Eyo Willy Honesty mentioned in the diary. The custom no longer survives among the Efik. However, an analogous custom apparently occurs among the inhabitants of Uyanga Okposu, Calabar Province, who call themselves the Basanga.

42. Ambo is the name of an extended family of Creek Town known in Efik as *Mbarakom*. Feuds between the Ambo family and the Eyo Honesty family frequently resulted in internecine battles. The Ambo family has the reputation of being stubborn and recalcitrant. Possibly the Ambo originated from the Ekoi.

43. The drum referred to here is most probably a small wooden drum with a skin-head, on which are painted various *nsibidi*, or secret signs intelligible only to members of the Ekpe Society. A creditor could appeal to the Society to obtain payment from a debtor. A messenger carries the drum to the

72 EFIK TRADERS OF OLD CALABAR

debtor together with a message summoning him to appear at the palaver shed for adjudication of the case. The appearance of the drum with *nsibidi* signifies the importance and trustworthiness of the messenger.

44. The Efik word *ɔbɔŋ* means 'chief'. Here it refers to the chiefs of the different Ekpe Society grades.

45. Willy Honesty's town is Creek Town, known in Efik as *obio oko*, 'that town', *esik edik*, 'net of creek', and *ekuritonko*. The last is probably of Efut origin.

46. The word *ɔfiɔŋ* means 'moon', and is used as a personal name as well as a euphemism for menstruation. The Efik have an eight-day week, which consists of four day names repeated in two cycles and distinguished by the adjectives *akwa*, 'big', and *ekpri*, 'small'. Efik personal names may be based on the day the individual was born. Thus, a man born on *Akwa ɔfiɔŋ* or *Ekpri ɔfiɔŋ* may be named *Efiɔŋ* or *Ɔfiɔŋ* and a woman *Afiɔŋ*.

47. Duke Town is situated about twenty miles from the Calabar River estuary. Ships anchored off Parrot Island and took in a native pilot. Holman (1840, p. 358) in 1828 voyaged to Calabar and the ship in which he was a passenger anchored off Parrot Island until the Duke's head pilot came aboard to steer it past the various islands and mud flats. At the present time most large steamships dispense with a pilot, since their Captains are familiar with the approach to the port.

48. The Andoni live on the creeks on the north side of the Calabar River estuary. According to Westermann and Bryan (1952, p. 133), the Andoni speak a dialect of the Ibibio-Efik cluster.

49. The Efik possess a magic liquid known as *mbiam* which will kill anyone who swears a false oath (see p. 20). Each individual swears an *mbiam* oath that he will refrain from cheating the other on penalty of sickness or death caused by the oath medicine. The form of the oath is usually: 'If I do such-and-such, *mbiam*, you kill me.'

50. Archibong is an anglicization of the Efik name, *Asibɔŋ*.

NOTES ON THE DIARY 73

51. Williams (1897, pp. 547-8) gives the contents of a letter written in 1773 from Robin John Otto Ephraim to Captain Ambrose Lace in which a Captain Cooper is mentioned.

52. In December, 1778, during the American War of Independence, Captain Fairweather in the *Bellona* captured a schooner loaded with seventy-five hogsheads of tobacco. In December 1781 he sank the *Nelly* in the Grand Canaries with a cargo of 429 slaves, and one of the crew perished (see Williams, 1897, pp. 227, 566).

53. A 'bad day' to an Efik is a day on which trouble or sadness occurs. In connection with 'good' and 'bad' days, the Efik believe that the first person seen on a day foretells whether one will have a happy or bad day. Those persons who bring an unlucky day are called *idiɔk okut usen*, 'bad sight day', and are usually enemies. Such a person is feared, and if his voice is heard outside the house one usually remains inside to avoid seeing him.

54. See p. 22.

55. 'Pocket Honesty' denotes a handkerchief or head-tie, so called because the colour was unfading and thus 'honest', or because the trade article was first introduced via Eyo Willy Honesty of Creek Town. The modern Efik word *bɔkit*, 'head-tie', derives from the English 'pocket', probably an abbreviation of 'pocket-handkerchief'.

56. Unfortunately, the native name or nature of the play is unspecified. Most probably it consisted of a number of drummers and singers, but may have been one of several costumed plays. Presumably, from the reference to Ekpe, it was the Society's figure.

57. Hogan is the anglicization of the Efik name, *Okon*. Only a person born at night is named *Okon*.

58. Enyong is the name of several villages situated in the vicinity of Enyong Creek, a minor tributary of the Cross River.

59. The Qua, of Big Qua Town, three miles east of Duke Town, speak an Ekoi dialect and evidently held a feast to celebrate the arrival of the new yams.

74   EFIK TRADERS OF OLD CALABAR

60. Tom Robin, chief of Obutong or Old Town, decapitated several slaves to honour his dead son. The Efik sacrificed slaves at the death of an important freeman and believed that they accompanied him into the next world.

61. Grand Ekpe is *Idem Nyamkpe*, or the costumed figure of the *Nyamkpe* grade of the Ekpe Society.

62. See pp. 10-11, for a description of such a meal.

63. The food usually served for initiations, &c., is *ukaŋ*, a dish prepared with large quantities of dried fish, yam, palm-oil, salt, and pepper.

64. The traditional Efik houses lacked windows. Slaves were never permitted to have windows if they owned a house for fear that they might observe some Ekpe Society secret.

65. A James Williams, Captain of the *Neptune*, obtained 350 slaves from Old Calabar in 1799 (Williams, 1897, p. 684). In January 1769 Captain Williams of the *Nancy*, Liverpool, was plundered by natives at New Calabar after the slaves mutinied aboard his ship (Williams, 1897, p. 549).

65a. The name of a fishing village, as well as Tom Shott's point on the left bank of the Calabar River estuary, probably derive from the name Tom Salt. All Efik-Ibibio dialects except Oron lack the *l* sound.

66. The Ibibio were called Egbosherry by Europeans in the eighteenth and early nineteenth centuries. The etymology of the word is obscure, but the first two syllables probably represent the Efik-Ibibio word *ekpo* (ghost). Barbot (1732, p. 465) refers to his brother's voyage to Old Calabar in 1698 and mentions a payment of seventeen copper bars for game to 'William king Agbisherea'. The word 'Ibibio' is derived by many Ibibio themselves from a reduplicated form of the verb root *bio*, 'cutting off a head', owing to the propensity of the Ibibio for head-hunting.

67. Old Curcock or Old Ekrikok is the Ibibio town of Itu on the left bank of the Cross River several miles below the embouchement of Enyong Creek. Itu is the present location of the world-renowned lepers' colony of the Church of Scotland Mission.

NOTES ON THE DIARY

75

68. The *O.E.D.* defines 'romal' as a silk or cotton square or handkerchief often used as a headdress, or thin silk or cotton fabric with a handkerchief pattern, and derives the word from an Urdu compound. In 1720 romal was valued at 11*s*. per piece; red-and-blue cotton romals cost 15*s*. in 1725, and in silk were valued at 25*s*. 6*d*. in 1730 (see Donnan, II, pp. 245, 324, 384).

68*a*. Women, children, or female slaves obtained water from springs. Probably the diarist's chief wife neglected to have the water-pot filled. Water is stored in a large earthen pot called *abaŋ ukpɔŋ*.

69. The ceremony of dressing an adolescent girl in a cloth signified the attainment of her womanhood (see p. 15).

70. For a description of a palaver house see p. 17.

71. Toother was the slave brought from Boostam. Presumably he had done something wrong, so his master sold him to the Europeans. Ordinarily personal slaves were never sold to Europeans so long as they behaved. A gentleman who sold his personal attendants in this way stigmatized himself as poverty-stricken.

72. Half-brothers (*eyen ete*).

73. An abbreviation of 'Grand Ekpe', or the *Nyamkpe* figure.

74. Evidently the chief of each town received comey directly from the individual ships. Why Henshaw Town should be included is unknown, since among the Efik a town must possess its own palaver or Leopard Society shed, which Henshaw Town lacks. Henshaw Town once attempted to build its own palaver shed, but Duke Town objected, destroyed the shed and thus prevented Henshaw Town's attempt at aggrandizement.

75. The *ɔbɔŋ*, king or town chief, was always buried secretly (see p. 25).

76. All swore an oath that they did not kill Duke by witchcraft or magic.

77. Williams (1897, p. 553) cites a letter dated 30 December,

76 EFIK TRADERS OF OLD CALABAR

1777, from Egbo Young Coffiong to William Brighouse and mentions (p. 254) that Captain W. Brighouse, in the barque *Swift*, was captured by the General Arnold privateer, Captain James M'Gee of Boston, in 1779.

78. Snelgrave (1734, p. 8) refers to his rescue of a boy in Old Calabar who 'was to be sacrificed that night to his god Egbo, for his prosperity' by a King called Acqua.

79. The Efik administer clysters by means of a hollowed gourd having a narrow, tubular end. The patient kneels with his forehead almost touching the ground, and his gluteal region raised. The herbalist—wife or relative of the patient—inserts the tubular end of the gourd into the anus, and pours the medicine from a clay pot into the gourd. The usual medicine used to cure constipation is *ibɔk ayiha*, 'constipation medicine', an Efik household remedy, prepared by grinding the bark of *Cola edulis*, the bark and fruit of *Mitragyna stipulosa*, the bark of *Conlaedulis* spp., and the bark of a tree called by the Efik *enɔi*. The mixture is rolled into a large ball, and a small piece is cut off, ground, and diluted with water when required.

80. The appellation 'Yellow' does not refer to skin colour but is a personal name which occurs frequently among the Efik.

81. If a ceremony is private to the Ekpe Society, all non-members remain within the house on penalty of being whipped or decapitated.

82. *Ekpe* cloth or *ukara* is an Ibo tie-dyed cloth in which blue triangles alternate with white; special *nsibidi* or secret signs (see note 43, p. 71) usually occur in the design.

83. The Ekpe figure must whip the widows and children of a dead member. Whipping may be mitigated on payment of a small sum, but at least one stroke must be given, even if the son of the deceased is himself a member of the Society.

84. Waddell (1863, p. 371) states that Eyo Honesty II terminated the funeral obsequies for his uncle Eyamba, chief of Duke Town, by shaving his head.

NOTES ON THE DIARY

85. The Ibibio are noted for their masked dancers, puppet, and stilt dances.

86. Presumably some type of cloth.

87. The editors of Crow's *Memoirs* (1830, p. 280) mention: 'At these executions the sufferers are pinioned, and tied in a sitting posture to a stake driven in the ground; and round their heads, so as to cross their eyes, is fixed a rope, the end of which is held by some bystanders who participate in the sacrifice. The executioner comes up with a leaden-handled sword, and generally at one blow severs the head from the body; when it is instantaneously pulled away by the rope, and, while yet warm, is tossed up in the air, and played with like a ball. If the executioner fails to strike off the head at a blow, the spectators set up a laugh of scorn and disappointment.'

88. A free-born man who committed an action which the Ekpe Society judged punishable with death could substitute a slave for decapitation.

89. The reference to the King of Calabar in this context is probably to the successor of the recently deceased Duke. King Ekpe presumably alludes to the headship of one of the Ekpe Society grades.

90. One of his wives who lived on a small farm and looked after his wine-palm trees.

91. The manatee is sacred to the Ekpe Society. The most prized whips carried by Ekpe figures are covered with manatee skin.

92. The diarist errs in his date. Possibly he alludes to his entry of 27 May 1787. Hanging is the usual mode of suicide among the Efik.

93. Unfortunately, the Duke's Efik orthography is obscure here. Possible *afaw* is the Efik word *ɔfɔ*, 'slave'.

94. Apparently a slave could claim sanctuary after escaping from his master if he broke one of the 'god basins'. Slaves when in trouble with their masters frequently fled to a powerful man and begged him to intercede for them.

95. Efik regarded the birth of twins as a dire calamity. They

EFIK TRADERS OF OLD CALABAR

killed the twins by putting them into pots and throwing the pots into the bush. Mothers of twins were usually expelled from the town.

96. Crow (1830, p. 277) mentions that the Calabar women wear large copper rings on their arms and legs, called 'mancelas'.

97. Slaves were frequently given absurd names as a joke.

98. Any disease which causes the body to swell is a bad disease to the Efik since it indicates the presence of witch-craft, the violation of an *mbiam* oath, or 'bad medicine'.

EXTRACTS FROM THE ORIGINAL TEXT OF THE DIARY OF ANTERA DUKE
1785-8

(on front page of Diary: antera Duke Ephrim.
December 24 the 1787. I be angiry with my Dear awaw
ofion I Did settle with him in January 27 the 1788)

18.1.1785

ABOUT 6 am in Aqua Landing with fine morning so I walk with Egbo men to go for Etutim (?) so his Deash 1 Rods & 1 small cas Bottle Brandy soon after we hav all Egbo men go to Egbo Bush Bush for mak bob about Egbo Young & Little Otto plaver so Egbo Young pay 1 goat & 4 Rods & Little Otto pay 4 Rods so all Egbo men com Down for Duk plaver and be join putt moony for 20 men all be 64 men putt moony 45 for Duk family 19 for another family

21.1.1785

at 5 am in aqua Landing with fine morning so I go Captin Savage for tak goods for slav

25.1.1785

about 4 am in Eyo Willy Honesty house so wee walk up to see Willy Honesty in yard so his killd 1 Big goat for wee soon after we walk up to see wee town & Did tak one great guns to putt for canow for two Egbo Young men Bring hom in aqua Landing so wee join to Henshaw Town and com Back and at 3 clock noon wee Everry Body go com to Deash Eyo Willy Honesty Daught. . . . 1496 Rods besides cloth & powder & Iron so wee play all day befor night

28.1.1785

about 6 am in aqua Landing with fine morning so I hav work for my small yard after 2 clock noon wee two go Bord

Captin Smal with 3 slave so his tak two and wee com back

29.1.1785
about 6 am with fine morning so I have work for my small yard all morning and at 2 clock noon we have go Captin Brown (?) for tak good for slav and Com Back

30.1.1785
about 6 am in aqua Landing with fog morning so I goin to work for my Little Yard sam time wee & Tom Aqua and John Aqua be join Catch men

2.2.1785
about 6 am in Aqua Landing with great fog morning so I going to work in Little yard after that Duke & all wee go to King Egbo for share Egbo moony for 40 men after that wee com way.

5.2.1785
about 6 am in aqua Landing with Little fog morning so I go Down for Landing after . . . clock noon wee 3 go to Egbo Young house Liverpool Hall for share 3 keg powder soon wee hear news ship com up so wee Run for Landing for gett 5 great guns Redy for firs sam time wee see Little canow Com & till wee his be Captin Loosdan Tender

14.2.1785
about 5 am in aqua Landing with great fog morning so I hav see my Boostam yams canow com hom with yams so I have pay Captin Savage 1000 yams for 100 Coppers and at 12 clock night Captin Brown Tender go way with 430 slaves

15.2.1785
about 6 am in aqua Landing with Little fog morning so wee go on Bord Captin Loosdam Tender and com back after 10 clock noon wee hear Loosdam Tender go way with 230 slaves

ORIGINAL TEXT OF THE DIARY

23.2.1785

... I go Bord Captin Loosdam for break book for 3 slave
so I break for one at Captin Savage so I tak goods for slav
at Captin Brown and com back.

6.3.1785

about 6 am in aqua Landing with fine morning so wee
have all Egbo men & Egbo Young go to Henshaw Town for
get Egbo moony after 2 clock noon see Duke send his wife for
call wee say Captin Loosdam send his mat to till Duk about
news ship com so I & Esien go Bord Captin Loosdam to know
so wee see news ship mat on bord so wee did ask him way
ship be so his say in pointstand (?) so wee com ashor and
7 clock night wee have all Egbo men com back the say
Henshaw Town putt moony for 19 men Cobham Town for
5 men one for Guin Company Egbo.

7.3.1785

about 6 am in aqua Landing with fine morning so I go
down for Landing after 10 clock wee go chop for Egbo Young
house Liverpool Hall and after 12 clock Day wee see news
ship mat com & com to till his will not com heer Did go to
Commrown so Duke say berry well may go way plase.

12.3.1785

about 6 am in aqua Landing with great rain morning so
I go down for see Duke I & Ewien in his plaver house soon
wee have Willy Honesty to meet for Duk with all genllmen
for new ship Captin plaver so wee writ to his for com ashor so
his say will not com ashor & wee 3 go on bord his for ask
him and his answer be & say he will not stay for us River
soon that wee com ashor and till all genllmen so the say
verry well may go way his plase to go.

23.3.1785

at 5 am in aqua Landing with fine morning so I goin to
see Duke in his yard so wee carry all wee yams & Rod for

EFIK TRADERS OF OLD CALABAR

Egbo yams for guin Company to share soon after see the Duke get his life from powder about one his yellow wife pip so all wee go to deash him copper for that sam time wee see that small Bristall ship com up again.

11.4.1785

at 5 am in aqua landing with fine morning so I go Down for Landing so I see nothing all day Butt 7 clock night I see two my poepls Com I was send to find Ephrim Aqua Bakasy & say canow over it for water and Loos Everry thing & canow all Loos.

12.4.1785

at 6 am in aqua Landing with fine morning so I walk up to market way and com down for see Duke soon after wee hear Duke was brow Egbo for one his son nam Egbo Abashey so that son no mind that Egbo so wee did go to Egbo Bush for call Egbo com and killd one his mother goat.

21.4.1785

at 5 am in Aqua Landing with fine morning so at 12 clock Day wee 3 go Bord Buowon so wee beg his to Trust slave to carry for pay so he will not after that wee com back and wee have Eshen Duke com hom from Orroup with 7 slave so I have my fishman com hom with slave and Robin send me 1 girl & my first Boy com from Curcock with slave and 12 clock night wee go to Savage

22.4.1785

at 5 am in Coffee Duke canow so wee get Longsider Captin Savage so we be join settle Everrything what we owe him so he Deash Crim (Esien?) 1 Big great guns and Deash wee so com way and Liv to the portsand.

30.4.1785

about 6 am in aqua Landing with small Rain morning so I have all Captin com ashor so I Little sick so I not drink no

ORIGINAL TEXT OF THE DIARY 83

mimbo all Day befor night I hear Coffee Duke killd goat for Egbo Young & Crim the play.

9.5.1785

at 5 am in aqua Landing with fine morning so I goin Down for Landing after that I see Duke mak Doctor for his god Bason soon after wee have great Rain Day.

10.5.1785

... so I be goin work for my Cobin after that I see Sam Ambo carry Egbo Drum to Dick Ephrim about Ephrim Watt send to Dick Ephrim for pay what owe about Captin Morgan was stop them

14.5.1785

about 6 a m in aqua Landing with fine morning so Duke send for call wee to go for Crim house for see what his pay to Commrown Backsider Bakassey head to be slave 560 copper for all so the did Chop Doctor about the will we slave for Duke so we mak one canoq carry them hom all obong men go to Willy Honesty town.

24.5.1785

about 6 a m with fine morning so I go down for Landing to go bord Captin Combesboch I & Esim & Egbo Young so wee hear news about news ship so not Bliv.

25.5.1785

at 5 a m in aqua Landing with fine morning so wee see Duke send for call wee com about Captin Osatam (?) want to go way soon after Duke & all wee go to Ephrim Offiong Cobin to mak Doctor for old Callabar Doctor for 1 goat and after 3 clock noon wee see Captin Opoter arrived and we hear Sam (?) (some?) Cooper in 7 father (fathom?) point so wee 3 go Down to canow.

26.5.1785

at 5 am in aqua Landing with fine morning so I go Down

G

84 EFIK TRADERS OF OLD CALABAR

for Landing after I com up to work for my Cobin soon after
I see Esin Duke Bring new Captin with him to my Cobin his
be the Captin Combosboch so his say ship in the porrots
sand (Parrot Island?) so wee 3 Did Drishst whit men and go
Down for his Boat & one Big canow to Bring up.

1.6.1785

about 5 am in aqua Landing with fine morning so I see
Duke son Run to till he say andony poeples catch wife the
Let no market go past want to stop men for old town plaver
so I send Esin go Down for Landing and Esin get his canow
so I get Coffee Duke so wee go Down two great canow and
Egbo Young Little canow two Cobham Little we go Down
soon after wee see them in 7 fother point so the run so my
canow first wee Run at them and the get way for Bush so my
canow get som time and poeples Run for Bush so catch them
1 men & two slaves in the canow & I tak the canow so Esin
Canow catch 1 men Egbo Young canow Ephrim Coffee
Brother catch 1 men so wee com home after wee get town
have Ebrow Optter Cosoin (?) to go Look them 7 men in
Bush.

2.6.1785

at 5 a m in aqua Landing with fine morning so I go for
Landing after we goin to Duke so Duke have mak bob with
Bakassey and at 9 clock wee have two new Captin com ashor
so wee have go on bord Optter 7 canow for coomy awaw com
hom with Dead slave for Orroup.

8.6.1785

about 6 a m in aqua Landing so wee go on bord Cooper
and com ashor about at (?) Done coomy soon after wee 3
send for see Eyo Willy Honesty about his no Drink Doctor
wee 3 send him 3 Jar Brandy after 9 clock night I see Esin
Duk come and till me about Arshbong Duk sister nam
Ambong his Dead his sick 8 day.

ORIGINAL TEXT OF THE DIARY 85

9.6.1785

at 5 a m in Arshbong Duke yard so wee have poeples mak groun for Sam yard after 10 clock wee putt his in grown so wee 3 firs 3 great gun and wee see Willy Honesty com to Coomy on bord Optter & Cooper.

15.6.1785

about 5 I Lig in my bud so I hear Egbo Young call out for me so wee 3 go bord . . . Cooper so I get goods for 50 slaves for wee 3 soon after wee com back

17.6.1785

at 5 a m in aqua Landing with fine morning so I go on bord Cooper and com ashor so I break book for 2 slave for Captin OSatam after 9 clock night I have send 5 my poeples for go Yellow Bellay Daught mother Dick Ebrow sister to stop one his house women to give ship sam as his Brother was give one my fine girl I was give to my wife and give Captin fairwether and his will not pay me that mak I stop.

18.6.1785

at 5 a m in aqua Landing with fine morning so I go down for Landing after I have mak Doctor for one goat at my father Bason.

19.6.1785

at 5 a m in aqua Landing with fine morning so I go Down for Landing with very Bad Sunday about what wee owe Captin OSatam after I go on bord Cooper

20.6.1785

at 5 a m in aqua Landing with fine morning so I go on bord Cooper and com ashor so I stop all Day befor 3 clock noon I no eat one thing to night I give Jug Brandy and 4 Callabash chop for Arshbong sister cry house

21.6.1785

at 6 a m in aqua Landing with fine morning so I go on

86 EFIK TRADERS OF OLD CALABAR

bord Cooper and Esin go on bord Combesboch so wee com ashor after 3 clock noon I have send pound with Esin to give Combesboch for get 8 slav to pay Captin OSatam so I Done pay OSatam for all I owe and at 7 clock I Did send my Brother Egbo Young for Boostam Trad for slaves.

22.6.1785

about 5 am in aqua Landing with fine morning so wee Captin OSatam (Tatam?) Drop Down in . . . Porrots iland.

23.6.1785

at 5 a m in aqua Landing with fine morning so wee have Duke go Down for Tatam I & Abashey Offiong one canow Esin one canow Duke one Canow all Captin to go Down so we get Bord in 1 clock soon after 3 clock wee Liv Duke on Bord and wee com Back with Tatam himself & all Captin

24.61.785

at 5 am in aqua Landing with fine morning so wee go on bord Combesboch so wee get slave for get Duke prown (?) and som to Ephrim Watt & Ephrim Aqua prown (?) so wee go Down with Tom Cooper and Captin of Combesboch tender and wee get on bord 2 clock and settle everry thing and his Deash Duke and wee 143 keg powder 984 copper besides . . . 3 pc pocket Honesty for wee 4 and Duke so wee com ashor

27.6.1785

about 6 am in aqua Landing with fine morning so I have Abashey Commrown Back sider and one his boy to putt prown for ship so I did go on Bord Cooper to putt prown so I did give him one goods so wee Drink all Day befor night Captin Tatam go way with 395 slaves.

29.6.1785

at 4 wee (?) a m with play for Arshbong Duke yard about his sister Dead so his did kill goat to us and after 10 clock

ORIGINAL TEXT OF THE DIARY 87

Day wee have Egbo Run sam time I see Egbo Young com
and call me so I did find him after word he say young Tom
Robin his Dead be sick 7 Day my Brother ogan & arshbong
Duke son go to Orroup

7.7.1785

about 6 am in aqua Landing with fine morning so go Down
for Landing and after 10 clock I have go on bord Captin
Collins to ask him what mak his mat Drop Down so his say
Captin Combesboch Beg him to stay Little time about want
get som prown out so I Did tak 2 Jar Brandy for I & Esin
and I did send Optter antera for Enyong to trad of slave

11.7.1785

about 6 am in aqua Landing with great Rain morning wee
have Captin Collins go river Barr with 230 slaves and at 1
clock noon wee go to aqua about King aqua chop new yams so
wee 4 carry him 4 Jug Brandy for Deash so his killd two goat
for wee 4 callabash chop so Egbo Young and Esin com hom
befor wee com for 10 clock night

19.7.1785

at 5 am in aqua Landing with small Rain morning so wee
hear Tom Robin family cutt men head of for young Tom
after 10 clock wee Duke and all Captin go Down for Captin
Brivon (?) plaver after 4 clock time wee see one new ship
com up so wee go bord him his be Captin Hughes com up
in 7 (?) an 7 fother pointt

23.7.1785

about 5 am in aqua Landing with small Rain morning I
have Cooper Capniner work for me soon after I see al Captin
com ashor for tak on bord so all wee go with King on bord
Captin fairwether for coomy.

3.8.1785

at 5 am in aqua Landing with fine morning so wee goin

88   EFIK TRADERS OF OLD CALABAR

in Duke yard for mak bob to Coffee Sam Ephrim & his wife
so Coffee Sam Ephrim sister com & fight with Brother wife
so Duke & all wee be Dam angiry about that fight

4.8.1785

at 5 am in aqua Landing with fine morning so I go Down
for Landing so wee have Jock Bakassey com to Landing with
ground Egbo in canow about Little time wee go Down with
two Egbo young Drum to fetch up and carry Egbo to Cush
and at 7 clock night I have all Captin super for my house.

14.8.1785

at 5 am in aqua Landing with fine morning so I have mak
6 Callabash of Egbo chop soon after 4 clock time we begoin
carry Egbo moony for Duk plaver house for share for all old
Egbo I putt for 3 men Esin Duke putt for 3 men Egbo Young
for 2 men Ephrim Aqua for 1 men Ogun Antera for 1 men
so wee have great rain for all night

29.8.1785

at 6 am in aqua Landing with small rain morning so I
go on bord fairwether to fetch his joiner for mak window for
big house so wee Bad Sunday beCause wee have Egbo Young
Offiong no well.

30.8.1785

at 5 am in aqua Landing with fine morning so I go to see
Egbo Young about his sick so I have Joiner work for me all
Day so wee super with all Captin to Esin house.

8.9.1785

about 6 am in aqua Landing with fine morning so I go on
bord ship and com Back so I have give King up Tabow (?)
Besides Chap so I killd goat and Deash him & poeples about
30 copper besides mimbo and Brandy so the play all Day
befor night so I mak Robirst Enyang father house to Drink

ORIGINAL TEXT OF THE DIARY 89

Doctor with Robirst and sent to trad heer for Enyang. All
Cobham town give Egbo moony 12 new town Egbo 4 for guin
company & old town Egbo

18.9.1785

about 6 am in aqua Landing with fine morning so I go
Down for Landing so I have go on bord Cooper so I find Egbo
Young so his tell me he say not one Captin be bord all go
down for catch fish with Willy Tom Robin so wee com ashor
soon and I have Esin chop for me & Drink mimbo

26.9.1785

about 6 am in aqua Landing with fine morning so I go
Down for Landing and after 5 clock I have go on bord Optter
I & Esin so Esin go way befor me sam time I & Captin Optter
see one ship come up in 7 fother pointt soon wee com ashor
& I run to till Captin fairwether so wee go down for Landing
and get canow to go down with Captin fairwether & Captin
Hughes & Captin Combesboch & Captin Optter & Captin
William all 5 Captin after 7 clock night wee get on bord his
be Captin Overton & Senders for Captin fairwether soon
after wee com to River & com ashor to super for my house
with them Captin and the go on bord in 10 clock with gret
rain.

27.9.1785

about 6 am in aqua Landing with fine morning so wee
hear Tom Salt or Captin and new poeples fight with Combesboch Long Boat Captin Optter Captin of Tender & Combesboch Captin of Tender in the Long Boat them was go down
for Look the Boat Combesboch poeples was tak for his mat
and get way with 15 good for slave so Tom Salt or Captin
Androw fight with them Captin so the poeples get Captin
out in Boat so Boat one Captin stop 32 (2?) men & 1 women
from them and Bring him soon after all wee go to meet for
Duk to know Duk think for Doe

90 EFIK TRADERS OF OLD CALABAR

3.10.1785

... so I mak goods for Callabar antera to go in Commrown soon after that wee 3 putt head togeter and settle what wee think to Doe and at 7 clock night I have putt thing in Egbo Young Big Canow & at 12 clock night I sail to go to Curcock.

4.10.1785

about 4 clock I am in Egbo Young canow in 7 fother Point so I see one Egbo Sherry fish small canow so giv the Drink Brandy and Did giv som fish after 2 clock time I have great rain all Day befor 9 clock.

5.10.1785

about 5 am in Duke Canow (Ditto canow?) in Tom Curcock house so I com up get ashor from Willy Curcock old market plase so I mak poeples get chop heer soon after com up and after 1 clock noon get from old Curcock Landing sam time I see my Brother Egbo Young & see bob & Apandam the com Down all one Canow so I walk up with 4 Rods 1 Case Bottle Brandy to Deash andam Curcock so I see Eshin

7.10.1785

at 5 a m in old Curcock Town with fine morning so I go Down for Landing so I hav apandam & my Brother & see bob go Back for Boostam soon after I did go to Enyong Creek for see potter mother house so I no find him in heer and I get for Enyong town & I see one slave soon after I have see potter nice (?) father house killd goat for me & Deash 4 Rods & 2 yds Romall so the & Callabar poeples give me about 12 callabash chop and get time to com Back in night because be so Bad Crik

10.10.1785

about 5 am in Curcock town with fine morning so I go Down for Landing so I hav give andam Curcock 1 slave goods to Live for his after 3 clock noon I have see us Boostam canow

ORIGINAL TEXT OF THE DIARY

com Down with 5 slave and yams in sam time I sail way to com hom with slav in my canow and 3 small canow besides my

11.10.1785

about 9 am in aqua Landing without sleep and wee go Down for Landing and I see Duke Sam Jack Esin about Combesboch Tender so he say his go way with 325 slave and wee have Ogon Antera and all wowo Egbo men the go with two Egbo in canow to Ebrow Ebgo Sherry fish men.

23.10.1785

about 6 am in Aqua Landing with fine morning so wee have go on bord Captin Fairwether Tender to get Tea to Drink after 11 clock Day wee have one foshin (?) Ebgo for brow all men and wee Butt Egbo Young to not comig and go to not way all Day befor 5 clock time and I have be angary with my Dear Awa Ofion about water so my mother com and putt word so his Did bring angary to my mother so I Dam more angary join about that

24.10.1785

about 6 am in aqua Landing with fine morning so I go Down for Landing so I see my canow from Landing so I see Duke send old Tom House to big me for send men to go catch cow for him so I Did go myself and I Catch for my hand soon after Duke hear that and his Did send me 1 Larg fish about that so I see tak Duke sister Daught for his house to mak were new cloth so all wee & Duke Did give abou 20 cloth and wee Did play all Day befor night & wee see Willy Tom Robin com to play with us & I Deash him some cloth.

14.12.1785

about 5 am in aqua Landing with great fog morning so I go Down for Landing for putt yams for canow after 8 clock wee go Down 3 Big Canow I & Esin & Egbo Young with 32

92 EFIK TRADERS OF OLD CALABAR

slaves so his keep 25 slaves and abou 6000 yams so his Deash was wee 3 great guns and com up sam time after 8 clock night go on bord Captin Fairwether to his Tender go way with 250 slave & 2 Town.

22.12.1785

about 6 am in aqua Landing with fine morning so wee have Esin go down for hughes so I Did send 2 canow for 1500 yams for 150 copper to pay Captin hughes his so Captin William go Down Captin William carry 169 slave Captin Hughes carry 480 slave

23.12.1785

. . . Captin Hughes his go way with 484 slave Captin William go his way with 160 slave so I & Esin go on bord Cooper for brek Book for 4 slave arshbong Duk son com hom for Orroup with slave

25.12.1785

about 6 am in aqua Landing with fog morning so I go Down with Drehst man and Captin Fairwether Drehst & Bring his Dinner from Esin so all wee to Esin new house Captin Fairwether & Tom Cooper Captin Potter Duke Ephrim & Coffee Duk & Egbo Young & Esim & I & Eshen Ambo Eyo Willy Honesty & Ebitim to Dinner for new year and Drink all Day befor night

30.12.1785

about 6 a m in aqua Landing with fog morning and I go Down for Landing so I find Duke in Landing & Egbo Young go on bord Captin fairwether and I have 5 my poeples to cutt Big tree at my Big Cobin after 1 clock noon I have Tom Cooper mat Mr. Charls com to me for nail my Bud Bottom on

31.12.1785

about 6 a m in aqua Landing with little fog morning so I go Down for Landing and I have see market canow go way

ORIGINAL TEXT OF THE DIARY

and at 1 clock noon wee go bord Cooper for dinner after 4 clock time wee com back

1.1.1786

. . . I have see Duke send canow for Mimbo after 2 clock time wee Captin Potter Bring his Dinner so wee have all Captin com to chop to Esim new house about new year wee see Eyo & Ebitim go to aqua Bakassey

2.1.1786

about 6 am in aqua Landing with fine morning so I go Down for Landing and wee go bord Cooper for tea and com ashor sam time I see all Bush Ebgo Ebrow to no man com up for house all Day after 5 clock time wee have see one King Tom Sott com from Duke 2 canow to stay heer for settle Egbo bob.

3.1.1786

about 6 am in aqua Landing with fine morning . . . so wee have Duke take goat & mak Doctor with King Tom Sott so fairwether send for men to Com on bord for tea so wee have chop for my house and wee play for Esim house & carry to arshbong yard & play at night

22.1.1786

at 5 am in aqua Landing with Little fog morning so I go Down for Landing I have send 4 hand for Little canow to mak my father Boostam misimbo to guin Company for com to mak with Ephrim Offiong about warr Copper and at 1 clock time wee Tom Cooper Tender go way with 383 slave & 4 Town.

23.1.1786

about 6 am in aqua Landing so I go Down for Landing after 8 clock I have my Brother Egbo Young & Apandam com hom from Boostam with slave Toother and wee see Tom Cooper & Captin fairwether the com up them was carry Tender Down in aqua River

94 EFIK TRADERS OF OLD CALABAR

29.1.1786

at 5 am in aqua Landing with fine morning so all walk up to King Egbo for work to plaver house soon after wee hear King Egbo Sam Ambo stop 3 Egbo Sherry men to the River about the was killd one his men and after 1 clock time wee hear Egbo Young Dear Brun young girl at Aqua Town

8.2.1786

at 5 am in aqua Bakassey Crik and with fine morning and I git for aqua Bakassey Cril in 1 clock time so I find Arshbong Duke and I go Longsider his Canow so I tak Bottle Beer to Drink with him and wee have call first for new Town and stay for Landing com way so wee go town in 3 clock time so we walk up to plaver house sam time to putt grandy Egbo in plaver house and play all night Combesboch go way with 639 slave & Toother

11.2.1786

about 5 am in Coqua Town so have Arshbong Desire me to walk up for Commrown with him so I Did and wee pas 3 Little Commrown town for way wee tak walk for 1 clock . . . to get Big town so the killd goat and Deash 1 iron 2 Rod for me so wee mak long time bob for th to Arshbong good so Did pay Boy slav and the Beg wee to Drink Doctor with them so arshbong mak one his father son nam Ebetim to Drink Doctor with him to the Deash one men cow to be killd & 8 Rod about that th Chap wee us so com Down in 6 clock night

2.3.1786

. . . Captin Potter go way with 284 slaves.

17.3.1786

. . . We com ashor and I Did tak one goat for mak Doctor at my god Bason. . . .

20.3.1786

. . . Soon I see Tom Cooper com up and say Captin Fairwether go way for Barr with 440 slaves. . . .

ORIGINAL TEXT OF THE DIARY 95

21.3.1786

. . . Duk call all wee to com for his plaver house to hear
Ephrim Egbo Daught with his . . . and Dick Ephrim and he
say will not marry Long Duk so wee find Everry bob be trws
(?) for him and wee hav Ephrim Duk women com and Break
Duke god Bason about he Will not marry Ephrim after 7
clock night I have my wif offiong Brother Dead by his father
yard and putt his 8 yds fine clothe Did putt his in grown in
6 clock time

20.4.1786

. . . I hav see the poeples about 200 hand com for mee the
want me to give 2 my father son for pown Roonsom the men
Eyo Duk was stop for what the owe him and the say one the
men Dead for Arshbong Duk hand sam time I see the first
the head men com & call me out to go up in the King Plaver
house to hear what they say soon after I see one my men
was Liv him to canow com up and tell me he say Enyong
poeples tak my canow way for Landing so I Run & go Down
for Landing I find no canow and the stop two my Boy out in
canow and putt for Iron so the com Back and stop awaw son
for my face and carry way to putt for Iron so the com Down
one time about 30 guns for the hand the Look for shoot me
and after 2 clock the Bring canow for Landing no be Little
time the tak canow Back and the keep me all Day without eat
any thing and after 9 clock night the Let me hav canow &
all my men Back

1.5.1786

. . . so I sail way to aqua Bakasy and I get the 1 clock noon
and I call for new Town first and I go to old Town so I firs
one great gun for Crek sam time I find Coffe Duk heer and
I hear Egbo Cry out in plaver house so I did carry 1 Larg
Cas Bottle Brandy & 4 Rods to Deash Egbo men and I Did
call the town genllmen & women and poeples to com & hear
what I hav to say so I Did settle everry bob and I give Coffee
1 Larg Cast Bottle Brandy & 10 yams so Coffee sail away in
8 clock night

96 EFIK TRADERS OF OLD CALABAR

4.5.1786

. . . about 4 am in aqua Bakasy Landing in Abashey offiong canow and I com way from in 10 clock time and get Jocket Bakassey town in 7 clock night so wee carry grandy in th plase owe me goods so the Did pay me 1 men slave for my goods so Esim tell he say the was kill cow for him & Deash 80 Rods besides 16 Rods for me

18.5.1786

. . . we hear John Cobham family mak play for the father so the Did cutt 7 men head of

21.5.1786

I have send 10 hand for work in Bush after 10 clock time wee hav Bush Egbo stop all men to no com up and I have Esim & John Cooper chop for my house Tom Cooper go way with 381 slaves

10.6.1786

we have Duk send all Egbo men go to King Egbo for shar soon Copper Tom Sott Bring for Little Egbo plaver so Egbo tak men tak 40 Copper for send Egbo sherry way & one goat be killd for them at 3 clock time soon see them two newsship com up Captin ford & one funchmen ship so wee go on bord them two and them ashor to Duk

23.6.1786

I see Duk send one Boy to com & call wee 3 so wee go & find Eyo Willy Honesty heer with Funch Coomy Book so Duk tell wee 3 to go on bord with Eyo so wee get Bord ship wee go Down to Look Book so wee and all Henshaw town tak coomy mor what the get for Everry ship we com ashor & chop for abashey

2.7.1786

about 5 am in aqua Landing with fine morning and I go

ORIGINAL TEXT OF THE DIARY

down for see Duke with Little sick 8 clock night wee all tak
2 goat for go mak Doctor with Duke

3.7.1786

about 5 am in aqua Landing with fine morning I goin to
see Duke with sick after 1 clock time all wee going to Duke
yard for chop them goat wee was mak Doctor and 7 clock
night Duk ferry Bad

4.7.1786

about 4 clock morning Duk Ephrim Dead soon after wee
com up to Look way putt to grown

5.7.1786

about 5 clock wee Done putt Duk for grown 9 men &
women go with him and all wee Look ferry poor Captin
Savage arrived

6.7.1786

... wee go on bord Everry ship 5 canow to Let all Captin
know

9.7.1786

... after 10 clock night I have Esim & Egbo Young &
Coffee Duke to com to my house to Look Duke Coomy Book
and think what to Don

10.7.1786

... all Cobham town genllmen meet to Gorg Gobham yard
with us family for chop Doctor with wee and com Back so at
9 clock time wee walk up to Long Dick Cobin with us genllmen
for Drink our family Docter

11.7.1786

... at 9 clock night wee have chop Docter with henshaw
family by Long Dick Cobin

98 EFIK TRADERS OF OLD CALABAR

18.7.1786

... after 3 clock noon wee have King Aqua Com Down with 157 hands and 16 women & girls and wee tell him for walk up to Gorg Cobham so wee and all Callabar genllmen go to meet heer for Drink Docter with aqua

19.7.1786

... wee family meet with Long Tom his be King aqua to Drink Docter with him and at 7 clock night wee family meet willy Tom Robin for Drink Docter with him

9.8.1786

... Esim till me he say one Bakassey genllmen was fear for com heer when Duke be Life now see him com and wee putt head together to carry his on bord ship for putt his for Iron and two his slav I was carry his on bord my self

4.9.1786

... about 6 am in aqua Landing with fine morning wee have funchmen Drop Down so Esim and I go Down with 2 cow and wee com up after 3 clock wee see 6 Captin putt head together and say funchmen tak one mat beLong to Brighouse Tender and one John Cooper whitman and 3 men beLong to Savage on bord funchmen the say all be 8 hand be on bord funchmen so all the Captin go on bord Savage and get all Ready so wee see Eyo & Ebetim com to till see about that and wee Did go Down all wee 8 canows to Big Captin funch for Let wee have then whit maen Back he will not let wee have them men sam tim wee see them tak Savage ship and com Down so the say the mush be fight to get them whit men so wee com up and Live them two ship heer so at 11 clock night Eyo & Ebetim he Did Drink tea in young Duke new house wee stay heer Little Long and Eyo & Ebetim go hom for the Town for let Willy Honesty hear that new

5.10.1786

... I see Coffee Duke send his son to till mee news about

ORIGINAL TEXT OF THE DIARY

new ship after Little time I hear 5 great guns firs in 7 father-
point so wee see ship come up his be John Cooper Tender
arrive so wee firs 3 great guns for him

9.10.1786

. . . so wee hear great firs in aqua River and after 4 clock
time we see one Tender com up his be Captin Johnston ship
will Tender of Captin Aspinall so wee 3 firs great guns

10.10.1786

I go to my Back Cobin for plants som mimbo tree and all
us family walk up to new plaver house and tak one young
Boy slave to mak Doctor and tak 2 guns for be firs for the
Doctor so one guns firs and Break for Long Dick Ephrim hand
Dick mush Loos one his hand by that guns

14.10.1786

. . . after 10 clock I walk up to new plaver house for work
and at 7 clock night wee have see Egbo Sherry send word
to know them Egbo Sherry Sam Ambo was catch 7 men the
come up for water abou 20 canow so wee send Egbo Drum
in to brow for all abou town to no com go to market in soon
morning I send and am nothing to one good canow go up in
Curock River to tak car my Cobin Boy

15.10.1786

. . . I think all Day about my Cobin Boy was go in Curock
for fear be catch and I can chop all Day be 7 clock sam time
I find his com hom

19.10.1786

. . . I have play aqua Doctor with one aqua men so I did
killd one goat for my god and Dinner with Captin Aspinall &
Captin of his Tender in my house Eyo Willy Honesty send my
Brother Egbo Young to Esim Duke about som Curock bob

H

100 EFIK TRADERS OF OLD CALABAR

26.10.1786

... I have putt water in my Bellay so I hear Egbo Run and I com to know I walk up to Egbo Young so wee see Egbo com Down & the Egbo men he say Sam Ambo and Georg Cobham brow for Captain Fairwether so all us family Dam angary about brow that and wee send to call Captin Fairwether to com ashor and Break Trad first to us family abou 15 slave and firs 3 great onshor and after 3 clock noon wee see Eyo & Ebetim com Down and Eshen Ambo so the want to Sam & Georg Cobham for mak the settle with Captin Fairwether

2.11.1786

about 5 am in aqua Landing with fine morning wee have all us family went to Creek town for mak play first for Creek town cutt one women slave head of one cow be killd and goat and firs 7 great guns so wee com back in 5 clock time after 9 clock night I have Esim Duk com to my cobin for break one punchon Brandy for share to all Duke and sister so wee have us cason go up to guin Company with apandam for fetch wood plaver house Drun

4.11.1786

I go on bord Captin Fairwether and I see Effie com up 3 canow and play Egbo in after the com up for Landing with Egbo so all men & all women cry for town for Duke I have my poeples to go wood 2 canow

6.11.1786

about 4 am in get up with great Rain so I walk up in town plaver house so I find all genllmen heer so wee get Ready for cutt head of and 5 clock morning we begain cutt slave head of 50 head of by the one Day 29 case Bottle Brandy 15 callabash chop I carry up to Everry Body and mush play for Everry yard in Town

7.11.1786

about 4 am in aqua Landing with fine morning so I did

ORIGINAL TEXT OF THE DIARY

mak all women Bring callabash for mak chop to give to
Everry Body and all Country play all Day and all night
all genllmen get to Dinner for Esim Duk

8.11.1786

... I see Jack Bakassey com and Bring one women slave for
cutt to my father and I have send my yellow ogan abashey
to market and all genllmen get Dinner for Egbo Young wee
news about new ship 3 head cutt of again

9.11.1786

... about 4 am in aqua Landing and I mak all women to
Bring Callabash for mak chop soon after wee have one TaEon
town cutt the Backsider town head of and Bring heer for his
Duke Play and I have all genllmen Dinner for me

10.11.1786

... after 8 clock wee have Bush Egbo men brow Everry
Body for stay to houses and tak . . . in 4 clock time sam time
all play be again to play all night

11.11.1786

about 4 clock wee goin in Town plaver house and wee be
again Drehst Town for Long Cloth & Egbo cloth & hatt and
Jacket and Everry fine thing and obong Egbo Run for town
1 clock time wee Don for that

12.11.1786

... I Did mak all women Bring Callabash for mak chop so
grandy Egbo beagain tak for women play all Day and night.

13.11.1786

about 5 am in aqua Landing with fine morning so I go
Down for Landing for Look plase to mak Dwelld house soon
after that wee have all Egbo men mak Duke all women for pay
5 5 copper for Egbo after 8 clock night wee have all Egbo

102 EFIK TRADERS OF OLD CALABAR

poeples meet for Plaver house and mak all Duke wife to com and cry Egbo cry in town plaver house

8.12.1786

... I go Down for Landing to get all great guns Ready and wee have firs 28 great guns for ashor one one for everry ship about wee shave head first and wer fine hatt & fine clothe & Hanschiff so all Captin and wee genllmen get Dinner for Esim house

9.12.1786

about 6 am in aqua Landing with small fog morning and I walk up to see Egbo Sherry play wee wer new cloth and at 12 clock night Captin Fairwether Tender go way with 280 slaves

19.12.1786

... I walk up to Esim and Egbo Young and Esim play with one Country poeples Liv abou Guin Company sides the was com to see us about Duke Dead after that wee have go on bord ship and after 12 clock night Captin Brikhouse Tender go way with 420 slaves

24.12.1786

... wee have Egbo Run for abou town and after 7 clock night wee Read Letter com to Willy Honesty about what Egbo monny the putt for Willy & Tom Curcock 40 men first and 13 men mor for Cobham family in aqua Landing that

25.12.1786

about 5 am in aqua Landing so I have Drehst & Esim & Egbo Young so Esim & Egbo Young canow go to Boostam and after 1 clock noon wee have all Captin Drehst and com ashor to Dinner for Esim Duke house with us genllmen and Willy Tom Robin

28.12.1786

... so wee have meet all us family for Young Tom Curcock

ORIGINAL TEXT OF THE DIARY 103

about his say he say Duke was owe his father 2 Bx Rods and 3 slave so all us family find his be Dam Lye

1.1.1787

about 5 am in aqua Landing with small fog morning so I have mak 8 Callabash Egbo chop and 1 clock time all Captin and us get Dinner for Egbo Young house Liverpool Hall 3 clock time wee have putt monny for 17 men to be Callabar Egbo

24.1.1787

. . . so I see Egbo Young send one his men to com and call me so all Duke family walk up to Egbo Young house and see have mak great bob about Egbo so I and Ephrim aqua bring Little angary word to him & I for som word his speak about my father Willy Tom Robin pay mor Egbo moony Long Duke mor Egbo moony belong to Imo (?) Duk son willy Honesty and Cobham family give old town Egbo moony for 41 men.

31.1.1787

. . . so I walk up Esim & Egbo Young after we hear aqua Bakassey be for River so I & Egbo Young go Down for Landing to see and 12 clock time wee see old town com so wee go Down to fetch them up and see Did putt moony for 51 men Henshaw town putt for 8 men Willy Tom for one all be 60 men the Catch for wee and 7 clock night the goin hom

1.2.1787

. . . at 7 clock night wee have Captin Aspinall Tender go his way with 300 slaves

2.2.1787

. . . I see Willy Honesty play Egbo and com to my yard so I Deash him 1 pc Inder Roosnall (?) 1 g stuff 1 Rod for play poeples & 1 case funch Bottle Brandy 1 Long whit Bottle

104   EFIK TRADERS OF OLD CALABAR

Brandy after that all walk up to his for meet abou first warr copper

16.2.1787

... so Egbo Young & all Willy Honesty Drehst grandy Egbo plaver house so wee Did bought Egbo 344 men be Callabar new Egbo

17.2.1787

... at 6 clock night wee see Long Dick have som Egbo plaver with one Boostam men so all old Egbo be Dam angary and brow all new Egbo to sleep for Egbo plaver house

20.2.1787

... sam time wee see Willy Tom Robin send one his boy to till wee about one my Dear father son nam Ebo Dead by sick 2 Day so I have mak my Dear Awa ofion to go with 6 my men to went mak grandy 7 clock night my Dear com Back

22.2.1787

... about 5 am in aqua Landing with fog morning so wee walk up to see Willy Honesty so all old Egbo and I & Esim to meet for Egbo plaver house to know what man be old Callabar Egbo so all Egbo men find one Ephrim aqua son no be Town Egbo and one Robin Henshaw son and Henshaw Robin Henshaw so all old & new Egbo brow for them to not be Egbo men and after 8 clock night I & Esim Did carry 1 Jug 2 Long Case whit Bottle Brandy 1 Larg Jar mimbo up to Egbo house for give all old & new Egbo to Drink and Back 2 clock night

26.2.1787

... at 8 clock night wee have see Long King aqua send one his genllmen to be killd by wee hand so wee send that genllmen by Long Duk for River to be killd

ORIGINAL TEXT OF THE DIARY

3.3.1787

about 5 wee go on bord Captin Fairwether for tak Ephrim
aqua & Ephrim coomy and Coffee & Arshbong coomy and
wee com ashor with all captin so everry ship firs guns so
one great guns com up and cutt one Captin Tatam whit men
head off

17.3.1787

. . . so wee have Eyo & Ebetim & Eshen com with Egbo
to ogan poor Boy Egbo plaver so all mak his pay 335 copper
and one house Boy to Egbo Cutt head of soon after we have
them again hom

24.3.1787

. . . at 12 clock time wee have Willy Honesty call all genllmen for meet in Egbo Cobham Cobin for know who wee will
giv King of Old Calabar and after 7 clock night wee have all
us town genllmen meet for Coffee Cobin to settle everry Bad
bob we was mak sinc wee father Dead so wee kild 2 goat

13.4.1787

. . . wee have chop in Egbo Young house wee see all
Henshaw family com to see for ask us family for now to Let
the know who wee will mak be King Egbo so wee say wee
Don know befor wee settle about King of Callabar first

16.4.1787

. . . wee go to Creek Town 2 good canow & 1 small Dutto to
mak the guin company & old town about the 2 town want pay
Egbo in one Day so wee say never Been hear that for weer
grandy grandy father so willy killd goat for wee and I walk to
Henshaw town for see my mimbo wife and com hom in 2 clock
noon

18.4.1787

. . . wee have Otto ephrim and willy Tom Robin com to ask

106 EFIK TRADERS OF OLD CALABAR

wee if wee will to the pay first or the guin company first so wee say wee will for the be first and I have send my cobin for mimbo market

28.4.1787

about 5 I Lig in Bud so I have see Coffee Duke com to me and mak my Cobin Boy call me to him so his Did tell me abou amnaty (manatee) be killed in King Aqua Landing so I did mak 7 hand go with Jimimy Antera to fetch in aqua River so wee have been drink all Day to my girl wife in Duke sister Daught house

30.4.1787

. . . I have mak my ogan abashey to go up my father men mimbo plase for fetch mimbo so on after 10 clock Day wee brow to not men com up to no way and wee goin chop Bush Egbo in plaver house and I walk with Egbo Drum for Landing sam time wee Ephrim Watt no fear and com with 7 his men so wee walk Back in plaver house so all Bush Egbo men send word to pay 7 goat so his Did Copper for 6 great (goat) and 1 goat for that plaver

21.5.1787

about 6 am in aqua Landing with fine morning wee see Captin ford send his Tender way last night with 330 slaves so wee Done coomy on bord Potter and wee com ashor in 4 clock time

26.5.1787

. . . so I hear 18 men slave tak Boat and Run way from John Cooper Last night and 5 clock noon wee hear som them slave be to aqua town

27.5.1787

. . . we have see all Captin John family com to see about one the Daught marry Egbo Young was fight with another the wife and Break Toothes out so the com to Break another wife Toothes out again so wee Did mak Jimimy antera for tak Toothes out for the wife his Ephrim Robin Henshaw Daught

4.6.1787

... 7 clock night wee hear Captin Aspinall Dead so wee hear all pown cry out andam Ephrim mary Long duk

5.6.1787

... wee have all Captin ashor to Buary Captin Aspinall in Big plaver so wee have firs 6 great guns ashor

7.6.1787

... wee see Robin Tom King John and Otto Dutto Tom King John send them to com for mak play to Duke & my father and Egbo Young mother so the cutt one woman head of to Duke and 7 Barr Room men to be cutt for my father so the play all night

11.6.1787

... at 3 clock noon Captin Hughot & Combesboch and one Little ship belong to Hughot com from 60 slaves and one Aspinall mat Loos two his hand by firs great guns

15.6.1787

... John Cooper Deash Esim & Egbo Young 2 great guns and wee com ashor so wee hear King aqua was mak all his wife to Drink Docter so 11 wife Dead by the Drink Docter John Cooper Drop Down night about 8 clock time

15.7.1787

... Captin Aspinall ship go way with 328 slaves

18.7.1787

... so wee Sam Ambo beagain Cutt Cow for his god to mak play so wee see Eyo & Ebetim & Eshen send word to Let wee know the com to see Sam King ambo cutt Cow

108 EFIK TRADERS OF OLD CALABAR

25.7.1787

... I Did carry play to King Ambo yard about his Cutt Cow for god and I see Eyo Willy Honesty com sam time at 11 clock night I have com Back with my play poeples

26.7.1787

... at 3 clock time wee go to Cobham town to Everry man again Deash Sam King Ambo Copper about Cutt Cow for his god so His Did get 986 Copper for all Callabar so wee great Rain sam time and wee com Back with Rain all night

1.8.1787

... I com up to my work plase and goin to Egbo plaver house and I find Be som Body Tif Door out in Egbo plaver house so wee send Drum to mak all wee new Egbo to com in plaver house to fend about 3 Egbo for everry yard if will find

11.8.1787

... after 2 clock time wee have all Captin and Callabar genllmen wee have meet for King Ambo plaver house about one willy Curcock men was fight with one Captin ford mat so after Little time the mat Dead so wee mak that Willy Curcock men to be Cutt Ear about that fight

13.8.1787

... wee hear Captin Brighouse go way with 320 slaves

14.8.1787

... wee hear John Tom Henshaw Dead so wee Did send our poeples go for Henshaw town with apandam

18.8.1787

... I have Captin Potter com ashor after 11 clock time Potter send on bord his Tender & is ship to bring 35 whit men and at 12 clock the beagain putt 2 sides house up and after 2 clock I have all Captin Dinner for me and super

ORIGINAL TEXT OF THE DIARY 109

25.8.1787

... at 4 clock noon wee have Captin fairweather Tender go way with 210 slaves.

31.8.1787

... I hear one John Tom Cobham wife be Hang himself about (woman) plaver October 17th the 1787

Jimimy Henshaw pay his for 4 Callabar Laws (afaws?) for be King Egbo.

Willy Honesty	. .	20 Rods & one goat
Georg old town	. .	10 Rods
Tom Nonaw	. .	10 Rods
old & new Egbo	. .	8 Rods
Robin Curcock	. .	5 Rods
Guin Company	.	
King Egbo	. .	5 Rods
Eyamba	. .	10 Rods
old & new Egbo	. .	8 Rods
Tom Cobham	. .	10 Rods
Duk Ephrim	. .	20 Rods & goat
Egbo Young Offion	.	25 Rods & goat
Robin John	. .	5 Rods
John Ambo	. .	5 Rods
Willy Tom	. .	4 Rods
Tom Curcock	. .	5 Rods
old & new Egbo	. .	8 Rods
Effar	. .	5 Rods
Misimbo	. .	4 Rods
King Ambo	. .	20 Rods & goat
Ephrim Aqua	. .	5 Rods

5.9.1787

... so wee carry Egbo in King Ambo about one Tatam pown was Run way so wee mak is give one his son for Tatam

110 EFIK TRADERS OF OLD CALABAR

16.9.1787

... wee tak grandy Egbo and carry to Henshaw & Willy tom for brow for not Captin for send any Callabar poun was putt for tak my slave goods to not send them poun way in Tender so wee have Tatam Tender go way with 330 slaves

19.9.1787

... after 12 clock Day wee get Dinner in my house and Drink fine mimbo so wee hear one guns firs so we mak 2 . .3 Boy Run to go know who firs guns so them Boys com Back and till wee he say my yellow ogan abashey shoot his wife for guns so shot not Toutch

20.9.1787

... I see my yellow ogan abashey wife nam Eba com to me and he say chop Docter and I send my Dear so my Dear send word he say his vomit so I tell my Dear for carry him to my mother for giv mor Docter for Drink and I go on bord after so wee see my mother send word to me he say his be Dead my yellow ogan wife soon we have one Little snow Brsh ship was in Comrown so com to get som sail and I have Carpnter beagain Lay floor new house first Day

Here is written in   Antera Duke Ejus Liber
another hand   Archibald Forrest   Thomas Taylor

26.9.1787

... about 6 am in aqua Landing with fine morning his Day wee have 9 ship in River so wee have willy Honesty and all us go on bord snow Brsh ship for settle coomy plaver so his will pay 1000 copper for Everry Callabar Old Otto Duk Daught Drink Docter with Husbun wife

1.10.1787

... I have see two King aqua women slave com from my yard Break one my god Bason he say will be slave so I Did

ORIGINAL TEXT OF THE DIARY

send word to King aqua to Let us know and after 2 clock wee
all 4 Callabar new & old Egbo go to meet to King Ambo
plaver house about willy Curcock Egbo plaver

3.10.1787

. . . His Day wee 10 ship in River so I have send my cobin
boy Eyo Ebrow son in mimbo market soon after wee hear new
ship in portsan

9.10.1787

. . . wee see Willy Honesty send to wee for com on bord
Rogers to meet so wee mak 500 coppers to give Robin John
for his coomy for hav nam for Coomy Book

17.10.1787

. . . I walk up to Egbo Young and Esim and after wee com
Down for my house and send my Cobin Boy for apandam
Cobin to goin Bring 115 BeLong to Jimimy so wee begain
shar for all 4 Callabar Egbo to mak Jimimy Henshaw to be
King Egbo

22.10.1787

. . . wee hear all Creek town genllmen com with Willy
Honesty to King Ambo so all wee and men & women Did go
to King Ambo plaver house so Willy send on bord Captin
Fairweather to goin call Coffee Duk so his Did com ashor
with Captin fairweather and so Callabar beagain ask him
what mak Been Run way on Bord after word he say his hear
wee 4 was Drink Docter to killd him so wee tell Callabar wee
was Drink Docter to not one we go to his house because wee
hear Duke Sister he say be his killd Duke and to Let his Drink
Docter with Duke Sister before wee settle sam time wee have
send to call Duke Sister so his Did com to plaver house after-
word he beagain Bring all bob to all Callabar . . . and he say
want to Drink Docter with Coffee so Everry Body ask Coffee
to Drink Docter with him so Coffee will not Drink Docter

112 EFIK TRADERS OF OLD CALABAR

so wee tell willy Honesty for send to 2 Egbo Drum to carry
Coffee to his house and wee say wee 4 will not settle with
Coffee if his not Drink Docter

25.10.1787

about 6 am in aqua Landing with small Rain morning so
I walk up to see Esim and Egbo Young so I see Jimimy
Henshaw com to see wee and wee tell him for go on bord
Rogers for all Henshaw family coomy and wee have go on
bord Rogers for mak Jimimy Henshaw name to King Egbo
in Coomy Book so hear all Captin meet on bord Captin
ford about ogan Captin Duk was fight with ford soon after 2
clock time wee com ashor and I hear one my Ephrim abashey
Egbo Sherry women have Brun two son one Day in plower
andam Duke wife Brun young girl in aqua town

1.11.1787

. . . at 12 clock Day wee go on bord Captin fairweather for
Dinner soon after wee have go on bord Everry ship to Let the
know I will go to aqua Bakassey to Buy Canow and after 12
clock night I sail way in Landing to agoin in aqua Bakassey
so I Did carry two Esim Duke girl with me and one girl
BeLong to my Dear that mak 3 girl wee 42 hand besides 3
girl for two canow

2.12.1787

. . . wee have see Captin fairweather Docter Dead so wee
have see Egbo Run for about Town

4.12.1787

. . . I have my girl arshbong Duke son sister putt Larg Rods
Leg mincles in Leg so I pay the smith 1 Rods 5 Boostam yams
& Jar mimbo

11.12.1787

. . . Tom John Cobham Dear wife Drink Docter all mush

ORIGINAL TEXT OF THE DIARY 113

Dead so I Did mak my Dear to go in Henshaw town to see him because be sister with him and Esim Dear go to see him at 9 clock night my Dear com Back so I have andam nothing com hom for orroup

13.12.1787

. . . wee have Esim send to go and see John Cobham in Henshaw town and at 5 clock wee 3 Brother walk up to Henshaw town to Jimimy Henshaw yard so Jimimy killd goat for wee and agoin for his cobin and stay heer and call all the genllmen for mak Long time bob and com back in 9 clock time

22.12.1787

. . . Potter go way with Tender go way with 350 slaves

25.12.1787

. . . great fog morning and at 1 clock time wee have Captin fairwer John Tatam Captin ford Captin Hughes Captin Potter Captin Rogers and Captin Combesboch and Eyo willy Honesty and willy Tom Robin so wee get Dinner in the Duke house and super so at 8 clock night the go on bord and wee Did firs 3 great guns

29.12.1787

. . . at 3 clock noon Captin fairweather go his way with 377 slaves

1.1.1788

about 5 am in aqua Landing with great fog so I go Down for Landing so I have mak my girl arshbong Duke son sister wer Cloth first Day and the women and at 1 clock wee have get Dinner with 6 Captin in Egbo Young house

3.1.1788

. . . I have go on bord to get som Brandy for two my Brother

EFIK TRADERS OF OLD CALABAR

and at 3 clock noon I have two my Brother and my Ephrim abashey the go way from orroup sam time wee hear Captin John King Egbo Dead in old town plaver house in all genllmen face

7.1.1788

. . . I see Robin John send one his old men to com and tell Everry Body is want go any Docter If be his killd Captin John King Egbo or not

8.1.1788

. . . I see one willy Honesty men com and tell me he say Coffee Duke he say will com heer to putt firs for all his house so I tak 2 Egbo Drum and brow to not men sleep for house sam time I hear andam Duk son Dead by Bad sick

9.1.1788

. . . old Robin Jno com himself and call Callabar genllmen go to King ambo plaver house and meet about the say be Robin John killd Captin John Ambo so Everry find that bob no be Tru Duk com hom for orroup

17.1.1788

. . . about 6 am in aqua Landing with fine morning so I go on bord ford and com Back in 10 clock time so I have Drink in my house 6 clock I brow all wawa (?) Egbo to again cutt firs wood in morning for putt to Town plaver house and after 9 clock night I have see firs get in to Potter antera yard so I go up in stop house myself & Everry men to Catch so firs tak 4 house soon after I see Willy Tom Robin com & Captin Tatam send one mat & 6 Boat Boy to help me

23.1.1788

. . . I go on bord to see Captin Potter about his cooper was Trun (drown?) for water Last night about 8 clock and wee have Combesboch Tender go way with 280 slaves and 2 clock

ORIGINAL TEXT OF THE DIARY

noon wee king aqua com to see Egbo Young offiong so wee
Did play all noon 7 clock night his go hom soon wee carry
grandy Egbo in plaver house

27.1.1788

about 5 am in aqua Landing with great fog morning so
I walk up to see Carpnt & Joiners after that wee have Back-
sider Drek Comroun com to wee with the new obong men so I
Did Dash them 4 Rods so wee have go Bord ford for Dinner

31.1.1788

about 5 am in aqua Landing with great fog morning so
I goin Down for Landing and I have send my son on bord
Hughes to call his ashor and give him slave and after that I
& Egbo Young & Eshen Duk agoin on bord Rogers at 1 clock
noon I have send two my father son for mimbo market

THE POLITICAL ORGANIZATION
OF OLD CALABAR

G. I. Jones

THE extracts from Antera Duke's diary which have been preserved give a tantalizingly brief account of life in Old Calabar at the end of the eighteenth century. But they throw considerable light on several features of the political situation described in the narratives of European travellers half a century later, when Old Calabar and Bonny were the two major ports of the Oil Rivers region, now part of the Rivers and Calabar Provinces of Nigeria.

In the period immediately preceding the establishment of the British Protectorate, roughly between 1830 and 1875, the basic features of the social structure of these Oil Rivers ports, in particular their organization into semi-autonomous corporate lineages, were much the same. Their environment and economic life were very similar, and they were all equally involved in intensive commercial intercourse with European merchant shipping, trading first in slaves and then in palm-oil. But their history during this period presents striking contrasts. In Bonny and New Calabar it was a period of constant warfare, and particularly internal strife, which culminated in the establishment in 1870 of a rival port, Opobo, by the defeated faction in Bonny and in the dismemberment in 1882 of New Calabar. In Old Calabar, on the other hand, there were no serious faction fights and no wars. But the handling of the large slave element in the population produced cleavages between slave and free which eventually resulted in the movement of 'plantation' slaves called the Blood Men. In Bonny and New Calabar slaves were completely absorbed and rose to the highest positions, one of them, Jaja,[1] being the

[1] A bought slave, said to have come from the Isuama Ibo village group of Amibo.

POLITICAL ORGANIZATION 117

leader of the faction which founded Opobo. European observers were equally shocked by the barbarities they encountered in all the Oil Rivers ports, but at Bonny it was the cannibal feasts following successful warfare that horrified them, while at Old Calabar it was the human sacrifices which accompanied the obsequies of leading men.

Historical documents and modern ethnographic data on Bonny and New Calabar are too meagre to provide any close analysis of their social organization, but enough material survives in respect of Old Calabar to present a fairly clear picture of the political system and to justify an attempt to determine the main factors affecting its very distinctive development. The most important accounts dating from the nineteenth century are those of the Reverend Hope Masterton Waddell and the Reverend Hugh Goldie of the Scottish Presbyterian Mission. These and other contemporary accounts are supported by the fairly recent descriptions in unpublished administrative reports on the tribal organization of the Ibibio. More detailed studies of particular political systems in the Bende division made by the writer were also found to be relevant in filling gaps and in elucidating some of the ambiguities in the contemporary records.

Outstanding events in the history of Old Calabar from 1788-1884 are listed in Table I (p. 118).

THE INDIGENOUS SOCIAL SYSTEM AND ITS MODIFICATION

At an early date the Efik came into contact with European vessels visiting the Cross River estuary and, during the eighteenth century, established a monopoly of the overseas trade on this river, which became complete by the subjugation, about 1800 or a little later, of the small Ibibio fishing community of Salt Town near Tom Shott Point.

The first accounts to give reasonably detailed information on the Efik date from the early nineteenth century and show that they consisted of three groups of settlements: firstly, those

TABLE I

Main Events in Old Calabar History, 1788 to 1884

1788. Duke Ephraim of Duke Town dies; 65 persons sacrificed at his funeral rites.

circa 1800. Duke Ephraim becomes 'the most powerful chief in Old Calabar'.

1820. Eyo Honesty I of Creek Town dies; 'over 200 slaves sacrificed at his funeral'.

1825. Eyo II re-establishes fortunes of Creek Town.

1834. Duke Ephraim dies; hundreds of slaves and others die at his funeral rites.

1834. Eyamba V succeeds as king of Duke Town.

1835. Eyo II crowns himself king of Creek Town.

1842. Agreement between British Consul and Old Calabar chiefs to abolish the slave-trade.

1846. Establishment of the Church of Scotland Mission in Creek Town and Duke Town.

1847. Eyamba V dies; hundreds of slaves and others sacrificed at his funeral rites.

1849. Archibong I recognized by supercargoes as king of Duke Town.

1850. Egbo law made against human sacrifices.

1850-1. Organization of Blood Men in Duke Town plantations.

1852. Death of Archibong I. Blood Men come to town to prevent human sacrifices and to watch the purge of Duke and Eyamba factions by poison ordeal.

1852. Supercargoes and Consul recognize Ephraim Duke as king of Duke Town.

1854. Tom Robin, head of Old Town dies; sacrifices of slaves and wives at his funeral rites.

1855. Consul adjudicates upon Old Town for breaking Egbo law. Mission suggests Egbo sanctions, supercargoes prefer naval action and Old Town destroyed by naval bombardment and landing party.

1858. Eyo II dies; Blood Men come to Creek Town; no sacrifices or other deaths and they disperse.

1859. Ephraim Duke dies; no disturbances and no sacrifices at his funeral.

1861. Eyo III dies; Blood Men again come to Creek Town and cause death of four people on charges of sorcery and witchcraft.

1871. Blood Men come to Duke Town on suspicion of Archibong II's death. Supercargoes cause Archibong II to send them home under threat of a trade boycott.

1872. Archibong II dies without incident. His brother succeeds him.

1875. James Henshaw declares himself king of Henshaw Town. Duke Town attacks and forces him to sue through supercargoes for peace. Henshaw Town burnt down and status quo restored.

1884. Treaty made between Great Britain and kings and chiefs of Old Calabar whereby British protectorate was established.

POLITICAL ORGANIZATION

at the head of the estuary called Iboku by the Efik and Old Calabar by the Europeans; secondly, a small group of settlements about ten miles up the Calabar River called Adiabo by the Efik and Guinea Company by the Europeans; and thirdly, the two villages of Ikonetu and Ikot Offiong on the Cross River called Mbiabo or Ekrikok by the Efik and Hickory Cock or Curcock by the Europeans.[1] Efik tradition, however, divides the tribe into two sections, Iboku forming one, Adiabo and Mbiabo being grouped together as the other. Ocean-going vessels were able to sail up the Cross River estuary and find a satisfactory deep water anchorage where the river which the Europeans called Old Calabar River flowed into it.[2] By the beginning of the nineteenth century Old Calabar had become, after Bonny, the foremost Oil Rivers port and by far the largest and most powerful segment of the tribe, with Mbiabo and Adiabo as its satellites. It had consisted originally of one settlement or a cluster of settlements near the present site of Creek Town. Later other settlements were founded (see above, p. 4) one of which, called Duke Town after its head, Duke Ephraim (Effiom), had, by the beginning of the nineteenth century, become the dominant settlement, a position which it has retained up to the present as the modern town and port of Calabar. The population of Duke Town was estimated by the Landers in 1830 as 6,000 people, which may be compared to Crow's estimate of 3,000 for Bonny a decade earlier. Hutchinson, writing in 1858, estimated Duke Town ('Atarpah') as being two miles in circumference with a population of 'at least 4,000'. This excluded the Henshaw ward, 'a small village having not more than about 120 inhabitants', and 'a quarter mile to the seaward of Duke Town', Qua Town with 'only about 100 inhabitants', and Old Town for which he gives no figures. He describes Creek Town ('Ekuritunko') as not more than a mile and

---

[1] Ekrikok should not be confused with Acrikok (Okrika), a fishing community near Bonny; see also note 38, p. 70, above.

[2] For the confusion which led to the use of this name, see above, p. 4.

120 EFIK TRADERS OF OLD CALABAR

a half in circumference with a population of about 3,000 inhabitants.[1]

Social Structure

The structure of these Efik communities at the beginning and again at the end of the nineteenth century is shown in Table II. It is very probable, although not certain, that the divisions into primary and secondary segments were conceived in terms of agnatic as well as territorial distinctions. For the social structure of the Efik is not likely to have differed from that of other Ibibio tribes as known in more recent times, except that the local communities tended to be compact and not dispersed villages. As these settlements grew into towns, families came to range farther and farther afield over the arable hinterland of Creek Town and Duke Town in search of suitable farm-land. Men spent part of their time in the town, engaged in river trading and fishing, and part living on their farms or plantations where they had settled many of their slaves. This pattern of residence differs considerably from that of other Ibibio and also from that of Bonny and other Oil Rivers ports. In the latter the population originally confined their activities to fishing, being settled on swampy islands unsuitable for agriculture, and obtained their staple foodstuffs from the dry land agriculturists farther inland.

Like most Ibibio the Efik had no tribal head or council of elders. The several local communities were held together only by common customs and interests reinforced by common rituals. There was, for example, as among most Ibibio tribes, the cult of a tribal tutelary nature spirit, Ndem Efik.[2] Innumerable kinship and economic ties linked together particular individuals and households in the various local

[1] R. and J. Lander, *Journal of an Expedition to Explore the Course and Termination of the Niger*, 1832, p. 318; T. J. Hutchinson, op. cit., pp. 115, 128, 133.

[2] The last priest of this cult came from the Cobham ward of Duke Town, but the office was loaded with so many onerous taboos and, in particular, one prohibiting participation in trade, that on his death in 1850 no successor could be found. Goldie, *Calabar and its Mission*, 1890, p. 43; Mylius, *Intelligence Report*, para. 32; see also above, p. 20.

TABLE II

Territorial Organization of the Efik Tribe at the middle and end of the nineteenth century

TERRITORIAL SEGMENTS

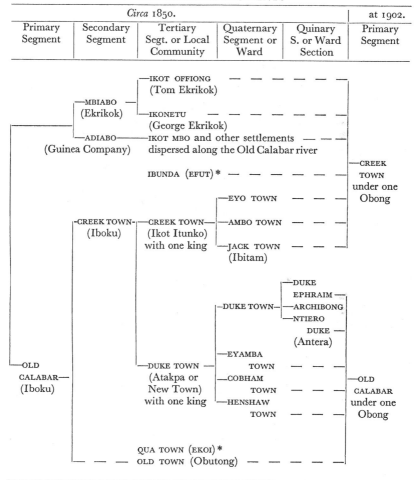

Circa 1850.					at 1902.
Primary Segment	Secondary Segment	Tertiary Segt. or Local Community	Quaternary Segment or Ward	Quinary S. or Ward Section	Primary Segment

* Non Efik settlements and original inhabitants of Old Calabar: Efut of the Creek Town (Ikot Itunko) area, Qua of the Duke Town (Atakpa) area.

122   EFIK TRADERS OF OLD CALABAR

communities. Each of these was, however, virtually autonomous and itself consisted of a federation of territorially discrete, self-governing segments which were regarded as agnatic lineages. These subdivisions of a local community can be termed 'wards' in a territorial, and 'maximal lineages' in a kinship context. Contemporary and later accounts referred to them sometimes as 'towns' (a word also used, however, to designate the larger local communities), and in other contexts as 'families' or 'houses', terms also used for various subdivisions of the ward. For these wards or maximal lineages were themselves composed of segments (ward sections) corresponding to major lineages which were spatially as compact and distinct as the congestion of the ward or the town allowed. The ward sections in turn were subdivided, according to their size, either directly into a number of expanded families or household groups corresponding to minimal lineages, or first into a number of ward sub-sections (corresponding to minor lineages). That the genealogical ties among these minor, major and maximal lineages were putative rather than actual will be explained later.[1]

The maximal lineage corresponding to each ward appears to have had a lineage head and a council of elders composed of the heads of its component major lineages and other householders of importance. But their authority was effective chiefly with respect to the external relations of the group; in internal affairs each major, or even each minor, lineage was virtually independent. The head and council of the maximal lineage had no authority to intervene unless invited to do so and then only by way of arbitration and for making peace. Thus Hope Waddell writes: 'If two equal branches came into collision, they might refer the case to the head of an elder branch, or accept the mediation of other equal branches; but

---

[1] It should be noted that the Efik of Old Calabar, as pointed out by Jeffreys (op. cit., p. 42), do not use the term *ekpuk* which, in the Ibibio dialects, connotes a body of patrilineal kin, but the term *ufok* which connotes a house or household without implying or stressing a kinship bond among its members. See also Addendum, p. 158. [ED.]

POLITICAL ORGANIZATION 123

failing these means of settling the quarrel, they must fight it out, till the weaker side gave in.[1] But the need for presenting a united front to other maximal lineages within the local community was usually sufficient, except possibly in the very large groups like the original Duke maximal lineage, to ensure the loyalty and cohesion of its component segments.

There seems to have been no council of ward heads exercising authority over the local community at the end of the eighteenth century when Antera Duke was writing, and certainly there was none in the nineteenth. Whether there had been such a council originally it is impossible to say. Most present-day Ibibio local communities have such councils, but they are very much smaller than were the Efik towns.

In addition to these Efik communities there were resident in the Old Calabar area two distinct and older elements, the Efut and the Qua.[2] These two groups formed sub-communities, analagous in size to the Efik wards but, while remaining associated politically and economically with the other wards of Creek Town in the case of the Efut, of Duke Town in the case of the Qua, they retained cultural distinctions which have continued to this day.

The expansion of overseas trade in the late eighteenth century, first in slaves and then in palm-oil, greatly complicated the relations between these series of local groups organized on a basis of agnatic kinship and residence. The simple economy was transformed by a considerable access of wealth and inflated by an excessive system of credit provided by the European traders.[3] Apart from extravagant consumption and

---

[1] H. M. Waddell, op. cit., p. 313.

[2] Not to be confused with the Qua or Qua-Ibo, a word used by Bonny traders for the Ibibio. (On the origins of these groups, see above, pp. 2, 4.)

[3] H. Crow (op. cit., p. 205) and J. Adams (*Remarks on the Country extending from Cape Palmas to the River Congo*, 1823, p. 245) both emphasize the difficulties caused by this credit system in Bonny and Old Calabar in the early part of the century. H. M. Consul Hutchinson in 1857 estimated that 10,000 tons of palm-oil valued at £460,000 were due on goods advanced by supercargoes at Old Calabar, while the yearly produce did not exceed 4,000 tons. (Talbot, op. cit., p. 204.)

124 EFIK TRADERS OF OLD CALABAR

display, there were few outlets for the employment of this new wealth, which was, moreover, very unevenly distributed. Able and enterprising men could build up huge fortunes so that marked social inequality developed between the rich men and poor men in various conditions of dependence on them, and Efik society became partially stratified into overlapping divisions of free-born and slaves, rich men and poor. This economic situation also introduced new and extra-teritorial elements into local politics, namely the supercargoes—the officers in the merchant ships responsible for mercantile business—the Scottish Presbyterian Mission, and the British Consul.

The Supercargoes

Out in the river were the European, mainly English, merchant vessels with their captains, supercargoes, and their European and alien African crews, the latter mainly Kru from Liberia. The ships came out with salt, cotton cloth, gunpowder, iron bars, copper and brass rods, and other commodities and remained there for upwards of a year till they had disposed of their stocks and replaced them with slaves or palm-oil. The Europeans lived in their vessels, roofing them over with palm mats, for the Efik were not prepared to allow them to build quarters on land. Trading was by credit, the supercargoes advancing goods on credit to those traders they felt they could trust, and in due course obtaining in exchange slaves and later palm-oil.[1] Each vessel was a small but effective independent establishment able to defend itself and, if provoked, to take the law into its own hands.[2] But the captains and supercargoes were, at the same time, vitally concerned to ensure conditions favourable to trade, that is, with the maintenance of peace and order. They could collectively, by threat of economic sanctions, apply considerable pressure to this end, but they had no means of intervening

[1] See above, pp. 4-5.

[2] King Eyamba himself was captured in 1846 and held in irons on board one vessel for non-payment of debts. H. M. Waddell, op. cit., p. 274.

POLITICAL ORGANIZATION 125

effectively in the internal affairs of the towns and wards save when invited to do so, as in the case of a disputed succession to the kingship.

The Church of Scotland Mission

A further European element arrived in 1846 when the Church of Scotland Mission established two stations, one at Creek Town and the other between Duke Town and Old Town. With their five or six European missionaries, their mission staff, school-teachers, and converts they formed yet another little self-governing group. They were able, like the supercargoes, to offer temporary asylum to political and other refugees from the Efik local communities, but they were not in a position to take an active part in the internal affairs of the two local communities.

The British Consul

Protecting the interests of these European elements was the British Consul for the Bight of Biafra, a post first established in 1849. The Consul was resident on the nearby island of Fernando Po, and acted during part of this period as its Governor. He could be appealed to in serious disputes between European and native interests, when he duly appeared in a British naval vessel to adjudicate. His judgements were accepted without question as having behind them, so far as the inhabitants of Old Calabar were concerned, the sanction of British naval power. This power had been effectively displayed in the movement for the suppression of the slave-trade, beginning in 1807 and culminating in 1842 with the conclusion of a treaty for its abolition made with the kings and elders of Old Calabar in return for an annual subsidy. The authority of the Consul gradually came to play a steadily increasing part in Old Calabar politics until it was eventually replaced by the British Protectorate of 1884-5.

The Kings

Whether or not the Efik originally possessed, like most

126 EFIK TRADERS OF OLD CALABAR

other Ibibio local communities, community headmen (*sing.* Ete or Obong (*ɔboŋ*) Idung) is unknown. But, in any case, among other Ibibio no powers of political initiative and no sacred status were associated with this office, which was merely that of the senior in rank of a number of ete or obong, each of them the head of one of the primary segments (wards) of the local community.

Early accounts make no reference to a single chief or head-man of Old Calabar. Barbot's account,[1] which refers to the period 1698-9, describes Old Calabar as being 'well furnished with villages and hamlets all about'. He lists as recipients of payments for provisions supplied to the ship *Dragon*, the names of Duke Aphrom, King Robin, Mettinon, King Ebrero, King John, King Oyo, William King Agbish-erea, Robin King Agbisherea, and Old King Robin. The use of the European term 'king' carried no implications of monarchy but was merely an honorific given to and adopted by the leaders of the Oil Rivers communities engaged in trade with Europeans. Grant, quoted in Crow's memoirs,[2] says that Ephraim preferred the title Duke 'which he considers higher and more expressive of power than that of "King" '. These names may all refer to people from Old Calabar settlements, or they may include some from other settlements as well. But in any case they suggest that there was at this time, and in contrast with Bonny in the eighteenth century, no single person who was regarded as the head of the Old Calabar communities. All the names except Mettinon mentioned by Barbot recur about a century later in Antera Duke's diary. Aphrom appears as Ephraim, Ebrero as Ebrow, Oyo as Eyo, and Agbisherea as Egbosherry, the last being used by Antera Duke as a personal name and also for the Ibibio people on the right bank of the Cross River. The only kings that Antera Duke refers to in Old Calabar are Duke Ephraim 'the King of Calabar' and King Ambo, whom he also calls King John and who seems to have been the head of the Ambo ward only. Antera Duke uses the word 'king' in two senses. First when

[1] op. cit., p. 465. [2] Hugh Crow, op. cit., p. 272.

POLITICAL ORGANIZATION 127

referring to the head of a local community or a ward, for example, King Tom Salt of Salt Town, and King Aqua of Qua Town; secondly when referring to an office or rank in the Egbo society, for example, King Egbo.[1] It appears from the diary that there was a head of Duke Town, who came from the Duke lineage and probably from its senior (Duke Ephraim) branch. Both in Barbot and Antera Duke this head is called Duke Ephraim.

Thus it would appear that during the eighteenth century the title of 'king' was assumed by the head of a local community or, in some cases, of a ward. During the nineteenth century, however, the associations of the title seem to have changed and the office of king came to be regarded both by Europeans and by the Efik as a distinct if alien institution. The number of kings of Old Calabar became stabilized at two, one for Duke Town and one for Creek Town, and they were regarded as the representatives of their respective towns in their dealings with Europeans. Europeans were asked to support their election and, by the middle of the century, it was the supercargoes and the Consul who determined it by conferring their recognition upon the person considered most suitable for the office.[2] The main importance to the European trading elements of the office of king lay in the fact that it was through the king that recognized rights to moor off and trade with the Old Calabar settlements were secured. It was also through the king that the local 'judicial' procedures described later could be invoked to enforce contracts and payments of debts. A list of the kings is given in Table III. Goldie, the only writer who refers to the method of selection, says that

[1] It is not clear whether the 'King Ambo' in one part of his diary is intended as an abbreviation for 'King Egbo Sam Ambo', or refers to another Ambo elder.

[2] Thus H. M. Waddell notes: 'This rank [king] is not native, but adopted to regulate the intercourse of the people of the country with foreigners. . . . As the office had special relation to European traders, they came to have something to say in the election of persons to fill it. This began with Eyamba [1834] who sought their aid, and has been continued by his successors, till Her Majesty's Consul has come to decide it' (p. 314).

128   EFIK TRADERS OF OLD CALABAR

'while the selection must be made from among the members of two or three leading families in Creek Town, always of the Eyo family, he who stands foremost in traffic and wealth is preferred in Duke Town'.[1] This, however, probably represents late nineteenth-century ideas as Goldie was writing in 1890. The list (see Table III) shows that the nineteenth-century kings were either heads of their maximal lineages or very close relatives of these heads, and that on the death of a king the office passed to a brother, or to a son, if there was one able and wealthy enough to take his father's place. In other passages Goldie implies that in Creek Town there was both a headman (patriarch) and a king, and that these two offices might be combined in a single person, or held by different persons. The accounts given by Goldie and Hope Waddell of the succession in Duke Town suggest that the office was originally held by the Duke maximal lineage, but during the nineteenth century was also held by the Archibong major lineage, while the Eyamba maximal lineage managed to secure the election of its head in 1834 and thereafter claimed a right to be eligible for the office.

The fortunes and relative prestige of the kings of the two towns fluctuated during the nineteenth century. The death of 'Old King Hio' (Eyo Honesty I) of Creek Town in 1820 left Duke Ephraim of Duke Town supreme and 'one of the most powerful chiefs on the Western coast of Africa'.[2] Creek Town fell on evil days and was without a king until one of Eyo Honesty's younger sons, who had attached himself to Duke Ephraim of Duke Town, was able to re-establish his own and Creek Town's fortunes. By the time Duke Ephraim died this son was sufficiently powerful to declare himself King Eyo Honesty II of Creek Town and he remained, until his death in 1858, the richest and most powerful man in Old Calabar. Duke Ephraim had meanwhile been succeeded as king of Duke Town by the usurper Eyamba V in 1834. On Eyamba's death the office was the subject of dispute

[1] H. Goldie, *Calabar and its Mission*, 1890, p. 136.

[2] Grant, quoted in H. Crow, op. cit., p. 272.

POLITICAL ORGANIZATION 129

TABLE III

List of Old Calabar Kings 1800 to 1875

DUKE TOWN	Died	CREEK TOWN (Eyo lineage)	Died
		EYO HONESTY I (Eyo Nsa or Old King Hio or ? Eyo Willy Honesty)	1820
DUKE EPHRAIM (Duke Ephraim lineage)	1834		
EYAMBA V (Eyamba lineage)	1847		
ARCHIBONG I (Archibong lineage)	1852		
		EYO HONESTY II (a younger son of EYO I)	1858
EPHRAIM DUKE (grandson of DUKE EPHRAIM)	1859		
		EYO III (Young Eyo, son of Eyo II)	1861
		EYO IV (Father Tom, elder brother of EYO II and 'Patriarch of the clan')	1865
		EYO V (Aye Eyo, brother of EYO II)	1867
		EYO VI (Ibok Eyo, brother of EYO II)	1871
ARCHIBONG II (brother of ARCHIBONG I)	1872		
		EYO VII (Ensa Okoho, relationship not given; appointed king and head of the clan)	1873
ARCHIBONG III (Edem, brother of ARCHIBONG I)	1875		

(Based on Goldie and Hope Waddell)

between the Duke and Eyamba maximal lineages. The mission would have liked to see Eyo II of Creek Town recognized as the sole king of Old Calabar, but the supercargoes preferred to retain a double kingship and tried to

130   EFIK TRADERS OF OLD CALABAR

by-pass the dispute between the Duke and Eyamba maximal lineages by recognizing Archibong I of the Archibong major lineage as king of Duke Town, with 'Mr. Young' (Egbo Young, or, in Efik, Ekpenyon), the brother of the late Eyamba V, as his 'prime minister'. Archibong I died in 1852, however, and the supercargoes and Consul, having again to decide between the rival claims of the Duke and Eyamba maximal lineages, recognized as king Ephraim Duke, a grandson of the great Duke Ephraim and the head of the Duke Ephraim major lineage. When Ephraim Duke died in 1859 he was succeeded in turn by two full brothers of Archibong I, who were known as Archibong II and Archibong III. In Creek Town the succession was not disputed. When Eyo II died in 1858 he was followed in quick succession by his son and then, on the latter's death, by a number of his (Eyo II's) brothers. It is clear, however, that none of these later kings of Creek Town and Duke Town were men of any great personality, wealth, or historical significance.

After the establishment of British rule in 1884, the succession to the kingship in Duke Town was again the subject of considerable dispute. In 1902 a Native Council Rule[1] abolished the title of 'Edidem'[2] or King and substituted that of 'Obon or Chief Paramount'. At the same time the secondary segments of Mbiabo and Adiabo were combined with Creek Town to form one division which was called Creek Town, and Old Town (Obutong) and Duke Town were combined into a second called Old Calabar. An office of Obong was recognized for each of these divisions, and the headmen (Etubom) of all maximal lineages ('families') included in the division were eligible for election to this office.[3]

[1] No. 4 of 1902 published in Gazette No. 1 of 31 January 1903.

[2] A Kwa word.

[3] '(2) In this [Native Council] Rule "Old Calabar" means Duke Town, which includes Archibong Town, Cobham Town (which includes James Town), Henshaw Town, Eyamba Town, Old Town, and their dependencies; "Creek Town" means Creek Town, Ikoneto, Ibonda (Efut), Ikoroffiong, Mbiabo and Adiabo, and their dependencies. (3) The "Etubom Obio" or

POLITICAL ORGANIZATION 131

In the nineteenth century the kings received 'comey', a fixed amount of trade goods and local currency which was paid by every vessel that moored off Old Calabar for purposes of trade.[1] Adams in 1823 estimated its value at about £250 and stated that 'a moity goes to Duke Ephraim the principal chief, the residue is divided amongst the minor chiefs.'[2] By 1852 King Eyo II was sufficiently powerful to receive two-thirds of the comey and King Ephraim Duke one third. In 1884, on the establishment of the British Protectorate, comey was changed to an export duty on palm-oil and kernels, of which half went to the Government and Native council, one eighth each to the kings of Duke Town and Creek Town, and one sixteenth each to the heads of Cobham, Archibong, Eyamba and Henshaw 'families'. Nineteenth-century accounts suggest that these payments of comey were used by the kings for their own purposes, but it is more probable that they were shared with the major lineage heads and prominent elders in the two local communities.

The degree of political authority possessed by the kings depended very largely on their wealth.[3] But the authority

Head Chief of each of the following families, namely: Duke Family (which includes Archibong and Antero Families), Cobham Family, Henshaw Family and Ayamba Family, and Old Town, shall be eligible for election to the post of "Obon" or Chief Paramount of Old Calabar.

(4) The 'Etubom' or Head Chief of each of the following families, namely: Eyo Family, Ambo Family, Ibitam Family, Ikoneto Family, Ikoroffiong Family, and Adiabo Family, shall be eligible for election to the post of 'Obon' or Chief Paramount of Creek Town. Native Council Rule Relating to the Election and Titles of Certain Chiefs among the Efik people. (Made by the Native Council of Old Calabar, the 2nd day of December 1902.)' Published in Gazette No. 1 of 31 January 1903, and included as appendix D in the Intelligence report on the Efik, Qua, and Efut Clans. The 'Head Chiefs' of the Creek Town division had little difficulty in electing as their Obon Eyo Honesty IX. Those of the Old Calabar division were unable to agree and it remained without an officially recognized Obon, though the majority recognized Adam Ephraim Duke.

[1] See above, p. 6.　　　　　　　　[2] John Adams, op. cit., p. 248.

[3] H. M. Waddell's accounts make it clear that it was his lack of wealth that caused the supercargoes to prefer first Archibong I and then Ephraim Duke as kings of Duke Town to Ekpenyong Eyamba.

K

132 EFIK TRADERS OF OLD CALABAR

even of pre-eminently wealthy kings like Duke Ephraim and Eyo II did not extend outside their own local communities; and even within them they were dependent on the support of other men of wealth and position. For in Calabar, as in Bonny, wealth was not concentrated in the hands of the head of a local community, but was dispersed among a large number of leading men. These men of wealth were drawn from all sections of the community, servile as well as free-born; some of them were close relatives of the kings but most of them were not. They might in some cases be as wealthy as or wealthier than some of the kings and certainly than many of the maximal lineage heads. They could, but only if their kinship status justified it, hope to succeed to the office of king or of lineage head; but however ineffective the king or the lineage heads might be, other individuals, no matter how wealthy, never attempted to set themselves up as their superiors or, as such persons did in Bonny and New Calabar, to divide the local community into rival factions.

The Maximal Lineage

An Efik local community consisted, as has already been said, of a number of household groups integrated, on a basis of agnatic descent and local residence, into the territorial units of sub-sections, sections, and wards which corresponded to the (putative) kinship units of minor, major, and maximal lineages. The basic subdivision of the maximal lineage was an expanded family which has been termed a 'household group'. 'House' became the local term for such a group, but it is also extended to apply to larger groups and in particular to wards. The household group consisted of the immediate family and dependants of its head and those of his adult kinsmen. Its core thus consisted of the men of a minimal lineage to which core other dependants, whether wives, kin, or unrelated persons, had become attached. It is, as has been indicated, tempting to assume that one could in the same way distinguish minor, major and maximal lineages as the agnatic cores of the sub-sections, sections, and wards, particularly as each of these

POLITICAL ORGANIZATION 133

groups is depicted as the agnatic descendants of an expanded household. But, as no attempt was ever made to remember real genealogies or to preserve distinctions between the descendants of true agnates and those of other persons incorporated into the group, one is left with the conclusion that, as in the case of Ibo and Ibibio lineages today, the primary function of this belief in agnatic ramification from a common ancestor was to provide a charter for the existing social and political alignments. The maximal and major lineages in such a system included all persons and minimal lineages that had, through long residence within the ward or ward section, come to be regarded as branches of the lineage. Lineage membership was also extended to the persons of known alien origin who, by reason of their incorporation into the households of full lineage members, shared the same interests and responsibilities as these householders. Thus, in this wider sense, the men of a ward and of a maximal lineage were almost the same, particularly in their relations with other maximal lineages. Hence the use, in Hope Waddell's and later records, of 'town' (i.e. ward) and 'family' as interchangeable terms when referring to the Efik system. Within the maximal lineage authority appears to have been vested in the lineage head and in the heads of other major and minor lineages, that is, in people assumed to be true agnates. But this authority was ineffective without the support of other men of wealth and social standing in the maximal lineage, whether or not they were agnates.

In the early period, that is at the beginning of the eighteenth century, the maximal lineages may very well have consisted almost exclusively of true agnates; but this was certainly not the case by the nineteenth century. In the same way, the household groups and minimal lineages, which formed the component segments of these maximal lineages, may well have begun as units of more or less equal size and status in conditions which limited their rapid expansion or contraction and in which their agnatic cores greatly outnumbered any other members. But by the nineteenth century the composition and stability of these household groups had greatly

134 EFIK TRADERS OF OLD CALABAR

changed and their cohesion into ward sub-sections (minor lineages) and ward sections (major lineages) was much more precarious and fluid. The households of able men rapidly expanded with many wives, male and female slaves, servants and other dependants. The households and household groups of the less able or more unfortunate men contracted. Their heads and other male members became dependent in varying degrees upon the wealthier heads of other households, to whom they attached themselves in various ways. Often they sought, by supporting one great man against his rivals, to improve the fortunes of their own dwindling household groups. Sometimes the men to whom they attached themselves were members of the same maximal lineage, sometimes of others and even of different local communities.[1]

By this time a lineage, either minor or major, no longer consisted of a group of freemen with their families, more or less equal in economic status, expanding only through natural increase, and with the wealth and authority concentrated in the hands of its most senior members. It now comprised a limited number of freemen with a very much greater and recently swollen number of economically dependent families attached to them. Hope Waddell and other authorities stress the point that the abolition of the overseas slave-trade and the comparative ease with which slavers could be intercepted in the Cross River estuary had left the Old Calabar communities with many more slaves than they could easily absorb.

Wealth, still a very necessary adjunct to authority, could now be accumulated far more rapidly and by the most able rather than the most elderly or the heads of large families. Some of the freemen were wealthy and in the position of

[1] 'Free men may become slaves in several ways deemed legitimate. *First,* By selling themselves . . . for protection, or to better their circumstances; as a rich, head slave may be better off than a poor despised free man. Theirs is a very mitigated slavery, and does not warrant a transfer of their persons and services by sale to another. Many free men in adjoining territories became King Eyo's dependants, or subjects, in that way, for protection against powerful and unscrupulous neighbours, who, they feared would kill or sell them.' H. M. Waddell, op. cit., pp. 315-16.

masters, others were poor and in the position of servants. Some slaves who had gained wealth were in the position of masters with slaves of their own. Their status was in many respects higher than that of some of the free-born. At the other extreme, slaves recently purchased had no rights at all and were simply chattels.

Most of the free-born, together with their household and trading slaves and their servants, lived in the towns, but an ever-increasing number of slaves and some of the poorer free-born lived permanently in the distant farming settlements —the so-called plantations. In theory every slave had a master who was responsible for him or her; in fact, the degree of dependence of a slave on his master varied very considerably. Wealthy slaves who enjoyed the confidence of their masters were virtually independent. Slaves living with their masters in the towns were more dependent on them than slaves who supported themselves on the plantations, and there were even cases where, all the free-born members of a minor or minimal lineage being extinct, the slaves living on the lineage farm-land were the only surviving members and were free in fact though not in status.[1]

EGBO

The maximal lineages, the basis of the Efik political system, were in no condition to provide, from their own members, a council of elders able to control the large communities of Creek Town and Duke Town in the nineteenth century. The European elements, though they exercised a continual pressure for the maintenance of peace and order, were powerless to interfere in the internal affairs of the native communities, and although the kings might represent these communities in their dealings with outside elements, there were no central institutions of government in the original Efik political system through which they could govern them. The institution on which, in default of other political machinery, they and

[1] H. M. Waddell, op. cit., p. 318.

136 EFIK TRADERS OF OLD CALABAR

everybody else depended, was the secret society whose real name, according to Goldie, was Ekpe but which was anglicized in the contemporary accounts as Egbo. There was no equivalent society in Bonny.[1]

Ekpe is also the Ibibio and Efik word for leopard, but there is nothing in early accounts of the Ekpe society in Old Calabar or of its modern survivals to suggest that it ever involved 'human leopard' beliefs and activities.[2]

The Egbo society of Old Calabar was derived from the neighbouring Qua who said they brought it with them from their Ekoi homeland. Egbo, as it survives today among those Ibibio and Ibo communities to whom it spread from Old Calabar, is a 'secret society' into which all the able-bodied men in a local community should be initiated as they come of age. Its esoteric ritual is concerned with the cult of a spirit of the forest whose propitiation is considered essential for the well-being of the community. There are occasions when the spirit is brought into the village and later returned to his forest abode, and the spirit has a number of lesser spirits as his servants who are represented by the younger members of the society wearing hooded or masked costumes of raffia or

[1] The indigenous term *ekpe* is used by Mr. Simmons in his Notes on the Diary, see above p. 66. [ED.]

[2] The idea of a man being able to take the form of a leopard, or of a supernatural affinity which could exist between particular people and particular leopards, is nevertheless common in south-east Nigeria. Goldie (*Calabar and its Mission*, p. 39) refers to an Ibibio 'fraternity' called Mfuro-ekpe, those who assume the leopard 'perhaps disguising themselves with the skin of the animal. Their practice is to lurk in the bush by the side of the road and spring out on any passer-by. A limb is cut off and the rest of the mutilated body left on the road.' In 1947 the name Ekpe was given to at least four different 'secret societies' among the Ibibio, namely: (1) Ekpe, an earlier society still surviving in the Ndokki (Ibo) area, elsewhere only remembered by the carved wooden heads worn in its play which are still preserved in some villages; (2) Ekpe or Ekpe Akang, a society of the Old Calabar Egbo type and diffused from Calabar; (3) Ekpe, a society of young men mainly concerned with the protection of farm crops, and (4) Ekpe or Ekpe Ikot, an alleged 'human leopard' society in the Abak division.

POLITICAL ORGANIZATION 137

cloth. On most occasions when Egbo or his servants are abroad, the uninitiated have to keep away, formerly on pain of death or a heavy fine, but there is also a public display and parade of the lesser spirits of Egbo which can be witnessed by everybody.

This ceremonial activity of Egbo was only one of its many functions. The Egbo society formerly 'ruled the village'. That is to say, the village elders were all senior members of the society and, until recently, enforced their authority and punished and disciplined the people in the name of the society, or rather, of the supernatural being to whom the society ministered. They could use its authority to support their legislative or judicial decisions, either by invoking the ban or taboo of Egbo upon the offender himself and upon his property, or by sending the agents of the society sometimes in their own persons, sometimes disguised as Egbo spirits, to levy a fine or, in the pre-colonial period, to kill him. These were its most obvious political functions, but even its more recreational activities had their political uses. The public festivals and parades, while satisfying the needs of the younger members for pageantry and display, also served to unite and discipline them. The weekly meetings of the society, which provided for the more mature recreations of drinking and discussion, also brought together in a friendly, non-controversial atmosphere all the men of importance in the community and constituted a forum for the peaceful discussion of village affairs.

Egbo in Old Calabar

The Old Calabar Egbo was essentially a society of this type, but it was modified in response to special conditions. Thus, to meet the needs of these larger and wealthier communities, it developed into a graded society with increasingly costly entrance fees for each grade. Only men of the highest grade could exercise authority either within the society or outside it. Holman, who visited Calabar in 1828, describes five grades, the fees for which amounted in all to 1,250 'white copper rods'

138 EFIK TRADERS OF OLD CALABAR

and 300 iron bars and were divided among the members of the highest grade, Yampai. Hope Waddell, referring to the period 1840 to 1860, says there were 'ten branches of various degrees of honour and power, some low enough for boys and slaves to buy as a sort of initiation, others so high that only freemen of old family and high rank can procure them. A person joining its highest rank pays an entrance fee to every member which . . . amounts on the whole to nearly £100, there being about a thousand members.'[1] Hutchinson, writing in 1858, says: 'There are eleven grades, the three superior of which, the "Nyampa", the "Brass" (or Okpoko), and the "Kakunda" are not purchaseable by slaves. In former times the Egbo title was confined entirely to freemen, the second or third generation of a slave born "within the pale" of an Egboman's dwelling being liberated by this fact, and allowed to purchase it after their parents were dead' (Hutchinson, op. cit., pp. 141-2). Antera Duke makes no direct reference to Nyamkpe or to grades in the society. But it is clear that a senior grade already existed in his time and that this grade shared the fees paid, for example for the rank or office of King Egbo.[2] The effect of this grading of members on a basis of wealth was that the authority which attached to wealth in Old Calabar could, for most political purposes, only be exercised through membership of the superior grade of Egbo. It also meant that the society in effect established a means test for those seeking social advancement and caused them to expend their wealth in a manner which was socially beneficial. For it gave to all men of wealth an overriding common interest in preserving the stability of the society and the social order of which it formed a part. Membership of Nyamkpe gave a man not only a pre-eminent social status, but also an assured income for life from the fees paid by those entering the grade. Any factional disputes, civil disturbances and other breaches or threatened breaches of the peace endangered these interests. They 'spoiled' the society, politically in that they threatened its unity, economically in that the wealth that

[1] H. M. Waddell, op. cit., p. 313.   [2] See above, p. 59.

POLITICAL ORGANIZATION 139

should have been expended on Nyamkpe fees would be diverted to other less profitable ends.

Little is known of the way in which the society was organized. Antera Duke's record shows that it included not only Efik but other neighbouring communities as well, namely Salt Town and Qua Town. Hope Waddell indicates that in his time it was divided into branches for each local community and also that the Creek Town Egbo announced new Egbo laws in Duke Town and vice versa.[1] But the Egbo writ, for instance in the matter of debt collecting, ran throughout the Efik territory, and a 'grand council' of all Egbo was able to meet and determine disputes between the different branches. Nevertheless, the essentially segmentary character of Efik social structure remained. No local group could be bound by any new Egbo law to which its Egbo members had not been a party or had not given their assent.[2]

It is clear from Hutchinson's and Hope Waddell's accounts that the second grade of Egbo, the 'Brass' Egbo, was responsible for law enforcement. The hoisting of the 'yellow flag of Brass Egbo' compelled all persons below this grade to remain indoors, and it was the 'sacred yellow band' of Brass Egbo that was attached to property sealed by Egbo.[3] Neither present-day Egbo societies nor the Old Calabar society had any elaborate hierarchy of officials with special duties and titles. Accounts speak of a head of Nyamkpe and heads of the subordinate grade.[4] In 1787 Jimmy Henshaw purchased the title of King Egbo for four Calabar afaws (see above, p. 59). No details are recorded of the way in which these heads were

[1] See above, p. 54; H. M. Waddell, op. cit., p. 422.

[2] This was the excuse put forward by Old Town for the human sacrifices which followed the death of their head, Willy Tom Robins, after this practice had been forbidden by Egbo law. H. M. Waddell, op. cit., p. 549 et seq.

[3] See below, p. 143, and Hutchinson, op. cit., p. 143; H. M. Waddell, op. cit., p. 503.

[4] Eyamba V was said to have achieved his election as King of Duke Town, 'having . . . purchased the headship of *Yampy Egbo*'. H. M. Waddell, op. cit., p. 311.

140 EFIK TRADERS OF OLD CALABAR

appointed or of their special functions, but it is clear that the emphasis lay on the equality of the members within each grade, and that no special privileges attached to positions of headship. On the financial side things were rather different; though a member could not improve his status once he had attained Nyamkpe he could increase his income by purchasing additional shares of the entrance fees. Holman, for example, writes: 'a Yampai may have his title multiplied as often as he chooses to purchase additional shares which entitles the person so purchasing to a corresponding number of portions in the profits arising out of the establishments'.[1] An example of how fees were divided is given in Antera Duke's Diary in connexion with the fees paid for King Egbo.[2]

What Egbo provided, and what was so conspicuously lacking in the Efik political system, was an executive staff able to carry out the orders and decisions of the senior members of the society. It had agents who, either as recognized members of the society ('officers of the society') or disguised as Egbo spirits ('Egbo runners'), carried out the orders of the society or of its senior members. With the weight of the society behind them, these agents could be resisted by an individual or a local group only at its peril.

The religious and recreational functions of the Old Calabar Egbo did not differ noticeably from those of present-day societies. The only special feature was the establishment of an Egbo day in the eight-day Efik week. On this day members of the society met together while the Egbo runners patrolled the streets and the uninitiated had to remain indoors and avoid coming into contact with Egbo.

The Political Functions of Egbo

Political functions were developed by Egbo to a degree never attained by other secret societies in this region. It brought together into a single disciplined organization all the leading men in each local community. Egbo, not a general

---

[1] Holman, op. cit., p. 393. [2] See above, pp. 28, 59.

POLITICAL ORGANIZATION

assembly of lineage elders, was the body that made the laws. In Ibibio and Ibo communities today, even in those where Egbo is said to 'rule the village', laws are only accepted as valid if they have been made at a general council meeting attended by all segments of the community. But Old Calabar was too large for such a mass meeting and these and other political functions devolved on Egbo whether its members wanted them or not. It was Egbo for example, which, in 1850 under European pressure, passed a law against human sacrifices.

Egbo again was the supreme judicial authority, while its agents acted as a police force to enforce Egbo laws and to carry out the orders of its courts. Egbo alone was able to execute distraint upon persons or property. Trade at Calabar more than anywhere else on the coast depended on credit, and the supercargoes' only 'legal' means of recovering their debts was through Egbo. To quote from Holman: 'When a person cannot obtain his due from a debtor the aggrieved party applies to the Duke [Ephraim] for the Egbo drums: if the Duke accedes to the request the Egbo assembly immediately meets and the drums are beat about the town, at the first sound of which every woman is obliged to retreat within her own dwelling upon pain of losing her head for disobedience, nor until the drum goes round the second time to show that the council is ended and the Egbo returned are they released from their seclusion. If the complaint be just the Egbo is sent to an offending party to warn him of his delinquency and to demand reparation, after which announcement no one dares move out of the house inhabited by the culprit until the affair is settled, and if it is not soon arranged the house is pulled down about the ears in which case the loss of a few heads frequently follows. . . . Capt. Burrell of the ship *Heywood* of Liverpool held the rank of Yampai and he found it exceedingly to his advantage as it enabled him to recover all the debts due to him by the natives.'[1]

Thus Egbo was the sole authority capable of maintaining

[1] Holman, op. cit., p. 392-3.

142 EFIK TRADERS OF OLD CALABAR

peace between different groups or of stopping fights and disturbances once they had broken out, since it alone could apply effective sanctions against offenders. In the same way it could intervene in the internal affairs of a maximal lineage to restore peace.[1]

During the later period of the slave-trade, when Old Calabar was filled with newly acquired slaves, many of them desperate men with nothing to look forward to except being sold overseas or used for human sacrifices, Egbo was able, with its runners, executioners and other agents, to discipline and keep these slaves under control. That at least was the native opinion; European observers were more impressed by the excesses committed by the Egbo agents in maintaining this order.

Egbo Sanctions

There appear to have been seven principal sanctions which Egbo could apply or threaten, either separately or in conjunction:

I. It could boycott, that is it could place an offending person or group under an interdict which effectively prevented any other person trading or having any other dealings with the offender. Egbo was 'blown' against the offending person or group, for example, against Adiabo and Obutong local communities, against a supercargo and his vessel, against the mission.[2]

II. It could seal the offender's property, placing its mark upon it and thereby preventing its being used by anybody until the mark had been removed.

III. It could fine an offender. A method used, for example, against King Eyo Honesty I, who was ruined and broken by being forced to pay an exhorbitant Egbo fine.[3]

[1] Though this was held to be an innovation and was done usually under European pressure; for example, Egbo intervened to restore order at the funeral of King Archibong I. (H. M. Waddell, p. 498.)

[2] H. M. Waddell, op. cit., pp. 448, 580, 591; Consul's report in P. A. Talbot, op. cit., p. 205; see also p. 30 above.

[3] H. M. Waddell, op. cit., p. 310.

POLITICAL ORGANIZATION 143

IV. It could arrest an offender and detain him or hand him over to the party with whom he was in conflict.[1]

V. It could execute an offender, either by simple decapitation or by fatal mutilation, the victim being left tied to a tree in the forest with his lower jaw cut off.[2]

VI. It could restrict people's movements and confine them to their own quarters by hoisting the yellow flag of Brass Egbo—a very useful power in case of civil disturbances, and used, for example, to stop an affray between the Ibitam and Ambo wards of Creek Town.[3]

VII. It could also use force by attacking an offending individual or his group and by damaging or distraining his property.

An example of the way in which Egbo sanctions were applied is afforded by the description of a dispute between Ikotoffiong and Ikonetu given by H. M. Waddell: 'The town of *Ikorofiong* came under the ban of Egbo in the following way: A man there sent an officer of the society to another in *Ikunitu*, to obtain payment of a debt; who, not receiving it, seized his children as hostages by tying the sacred yellow band on their arms. He did more, and exceeded the license of his order, by carrying off goats belonging to other people in the town. The *Ikunitu* people appealed to Duke Town, which took up their cause, and sent an Egbo with several armed canoes to repair the damage, by plundering *Ikorofiong*. The latter resisted, and prevented the landing of these unwelcome visitors, which provoked the Duke Town people to prepare for

[1] Consul's report in P. A. Talbot, op. cit., p. 205.

[2] H. M. Waddell, op. cit., p. 472.

[3] Hope Waddell records: 'A faction fight took place between his [Egbo Jack of Ibitam's] people and those of the *Ambo* family represented by Camaroons. . . . Hostile messages passed between the heads of the towns [wards], which ended in a street fight, the slaves on both sides being led on by their masters. King Eyo, hearing of it, hoisted the yellow flag of Brass Egbo over his house, and sent out a strong band of Egbo runners with their bells and whips, who soon dispersed the rioters. The streets were cleared by the time I got down and all parties were within doors' (p. 507).

144 EFIK TRADERS OF OLD CALABAR

war in earnest. All the proceedings were irregular; but King Eyo prevented the war against the offending town which had appealed to him, by calling a grand Egbo meeting to settle all palavers. *Ikorofiong* was condemned for having resisted Egbo, its fault being high treason; but was allowed to redeem its life by two substitutes, finally reduced to one head and a fine. We [the missionaries] endeavoured to secure that the fine only be exacted, even were it increased, and thought we had succeeded, and that the affair was all settled, when, after several weeks of silence the Duke Town Egbo suddenly appeared at our beach [at Creek Town], and, ere we learned what it came for, carried its victim to the old market-place, and took away his head. . . . Old Egbo Jack[1] asserted that no amount of money could redeem *Ikorofiong's* head; its offence could be purged only by death.'[2]

The Strength and Weakness of Egbo

The strength of Egbo and its value to the community lay in the discipline it could exercise over its members. It brought together in one single organization all the leaders and potential leaders in a local community. No free-born man in Old Calabar, however rich and powerful, could afford not to be a member of Egbo and thereby submit to its control; nor could he exercise authority except through the society and as a member of its highest grade. It was not possible, as it was at Bonny, for powerful men to enter into political rivalry with each other and to build up factions which split the maximal lineages and eventually the whole local community. Political feuds were against the main interests of Egbo which required peace and order so that its members could proceed with their business of trading and making money. Only thus could they continue paying the fees necessary for the Nyamkpe grade or, in the case of those who were already Nyamkpe, continue to enjoy the fruits of their investment, the fees paid by those who attained the grade. Some men might be so

---

[1] A Creek Town elder, head of Ibitam Ward.   [2] op. cit., p. 503.

POLITICAL ORGANIZATION 145

rich that they could ignore these financial considerations, but they could not go against the collective and organized will of the society. Nor could they rally behind them any group or faction opposed to the society so long as people continued to believe that the only way to social advancement lay in its membership. Thus, although political rivalry existed in Old Calabar as elsewhere on the Oil Rivers, it was never able to develop into faction fights, revolts or other serious breaches of the peace. By the control it was able to exercise over political leaders Egbo thus played a vital part in the maintenance of the political equilibrium.

But its discrimination against the slaves, the largest section of the community, proved a source of weakness in Egbo. By making a division between Egbo initiates, mainly freemen, and the uninitiated, comprising the women and most of the slaves, Egbo tended in effect to establish a class system with freemen subdivided into rich and poor, and a still lower class of slaves. In the words of Hope Waddell: 'Society in Calabar consists of nobles and slaves. The former are more than free, they have privileges inconsistent with the freedom of others not members of Egbo. Free people, too poor to purchase these privileges, if wronged, must hire an Egbo gentleman to bring their cause before an Egbo court, with a great fee proportioned to his success. Sometimes such persons prefer to sell themselves to some powerful chief, and gain his protection at the expense of their liberty. . . . [Egbo] seems specially designed to keep women and slaves in subjection. Wives, unless they have powerful fathers and brothers, may suffer the most horrid outrages from the most brutal husbands without redress. The only law it ever made for the protection of slaves was at the instance of foreigners.'[1]

The discrimination against women was of little political consequence. Egbo was merely recognizing a division that already existed in the Oil Rivers where, in any case, the roles of men and women were complementary rather than competitive. Women were not more subordinated in Old Calabar

[1] op. cit., pp. 313-14.

146 EFIK TRADERS OF OLD CALABAR

than elsewhere in the area and some women—in particular the mother or sister of a king or other important head—played an important part in local politics. But the division between freemen and slaves mattered a great deal, because Oil Rivers societies had not hitherto been socially stratified but were based on an integration of householders into social units which, in theory, were groups of agnatic kin and, in fact, corporate residential units. A man's position in these societies was, and still to a large extent continued to be, determined, not by his wealth in money or goods or by his status as freeman or slave, but primarily by the lineage to which he belonged and by the position which that lineage occupied within the structure of the local community. A man remained a member of a corporation—his household group and minimal lineage—and his wealth, though it might be expressed in terms of money and trade goods, ultimately consisted in the number of people dependent on him. The greater a man's wealth the greater the number of his dependants and the wider its distri-bution among such dependants. He might become the head, the 'managing director' of the corporation formed by his household group, and he might arrange for the greater part of his wealth to be employed within his own household or distributed to members of other households outside his own, whom he found it advantageous to attach to himself for economic and political purposes. In any case, however, his wealth quickly moved into the hands of a considerable number of people. The less enterprising of these were merely able to spend it, repaying the donor in various services which may be included in the general category of social support; the more intelligent were able to use and increase it to their own and the donor's advantage. Under such a system wealth did not remain in the hands of a limited number of persons to pass at death to their own sons and grandsons. When a wealthy man died, unless there was a son or brother of sufficient ability to take his place as manager of the corporation, most of the wealth he had accumulated disappeared among the large number of people to whom it had been advanced.

POLITICAL ORGANIZATION 147

Similarly it was possible for a poor man or a slave of ability, by attaching himself to a wealthy and able household head, to become almost as rich as his master and, if he continued to prosper, richer than his master's heirs, and the founder of his own household group and minimal lineage. 'Such an one at Duke Town, *Iron Bar*, by name, though originally a bought slave, became one of the first men, and most trusted traders in the town. He never was fully free, nor could he deny the claim of his deceased master's family on him; but they never asserted it, and no one else dare call him slave.'[1] Thus, there were great differences in the economic status and consequently ni the social status of freemen, and an even greater range of variations in the status of slaves. A slave, like a freeman, was a member of a corporate group and the longer he remained in it and the more closely he was able to identify his interests with those of his master and his master's lineage, the more his status improved both within the lineage and in the general community. This was naturally a gradual process, the rate varying in different cases, but, whereas in Bonny the process of absorption of slave elements into the lineage structure was complete, in Old Calabar a slave was never able during this period to attain complete equality of status with a freeman and the principal agency which slowed down this process of absorption was undoubtedly Egbo.

So far as free-born men were concerned, Egbo—though it gave to its Nyamkpe members an enhanced social status—did not allow them to transmit this superior status to their descendants; it made the grade open to any freeman who could pay the entrance fees. It thus prevented the development of a hereditary superior class. Indeed it did more than this. It effected a more even and a wider dispersion of much of the wealth of individual members of the community by providing for its distribution in the form of entrance fees among the 1,000 or more Nyamkpe members, that is, among men who were the leading members of most of the important household groups in the community.

[1] H. M. Waddell, op. cit., p. 318.

L

148   EFIK TRADERS OF OLD CALABAR

Between slave and free-born, however, Egbo sought to make a clear-cut division. It admitted slaves to those grades which were 'low enough for boys and slaves to buy as a sort of initiation', but it barred them from the higher grades. It also made no differentiation between chattel and other slaves. There existed in Old Calabar a convention that no person born in the place could be sold out of it, that is could be treated as a chattel slave. But Egbo disregarded such distinctions. In its view a slave had no rights against his master any more than a woman had against her husband. A master could treat his slaves as he liked (it was 'no matter for Egbo'), and so could an Egbo agent, in anything that could be represented as the maintenance of Egbo discipline.

THE BLOOD MEN

Origin and Development

By the middle of the nineteenth century, when they had become adequately incorporated into the local communities as members of the lineage farm settlements, the slaves developed their own organization in self defence against the arbitrary exactions of their masters and of Egbo agents. This movement came to be called the 'Blood Men' after the oath sworn by its members on joining, and Egbo was powerless against it. For the slaves greatly outnumbered the freemen and, since they were excluded from full membership of Egbo, it could not exercise the same discipline over them as over its full members. Egbo could pass laws against people banding together into such associations, but it could only enforce such laws by inducing the free-born to band together to suppress such associations by force of arms. The free-born, however, were not prepared to rally against these Blood Men; many of them indeed, including, it was said, the head of the Duke maximal lineage, King Archibong I, preferred to join with them, finding that they had many interests in common. For this movement was not, as the supercargoes and wealthy men of Old Calabar represented it to the Consul, a revolt of slaves

POLITICAL ORGANIZATION 149

against their masters. The movement began, according to Hope Waddell, in 1850-1 'among the slaves on the more distant Duke Town farms, the Qua River Plantations', their object being 'to resist the encroachment and oppressions of the Duke Town gentry and to preserve themselves from being killed on all occasions according to old customs'. Then, on a rumour that King Archibong I was unwell 'his people from the farms, many of whom had joined the "blood men" came into town to save his life. For that end they resolved that if he died, his native doctor should die too, and other suspected parties. It was reported that Archibong himself had joined their covenant to secure their allegiance to himself; and beside him, many free and half free people of Duke Town for their own ends.'[1]

The originators and the great majority of the Blood Men were slaves and not full lineage members, and the oath which they took on the mingled blood of their members and which gave the movement its name may have been intended to remedy this lack of agnatic ties.[2] But, whatever this oath may have symbolized, the movement was not organized by slaves to secure their freedom but was an assertion of their rights by the poorer, less privileged and mainly country-dwelling members of a maximal lineage or group of maximal lineages against the small, wealthy town-dwelling cliques that controlled, or more usually vied with each other to control, the politics of the maximal lineage and of the local community. What brought the Blood Men hurrying into town in their armed thousands was the call to avenge the death (always

[1] op. cit., p. 476.

[2] H. Goldie, *Calabar and its Mission*, p. 199, referring to the Blood Men in Creek Town at the time of the death of Eyo III in 1861: 'Ekpenyong Oku a head man of the town proceeded to administer the oath. He pulled up the skin of the wrist and cut it drawing a drop or two of blood which was mixed with that in the plate, and the individual took out of the blood one of the seeds which has a symbolical signification with them, eat it and then dipping the tips of his fingers in the blood, put them to his mouth . . . the administrator made a formal address to the blood charging it to look and avenge the violation of any breach of the covenant.'

L*

150   EFIK TRADERS OF OLD CALABAR

attributed to witchcraft) of a king or maximal lineage head, and to enforce the Egbo law against mortuary sacrifices (for which they had formerly provided the victims). The need for such a movement can best be understood if an examination is made of the tensions that existed within these maximal lineages.

Tensions within the Lineage System

The changed economic conditions already described had caused the maximal lineages to become more unstable and subject to far more rapid change in the size and composition of their component segments and in the political alignments of their leading members and their followings. The cohesion of the rapidly expanding households and their attachments tended to be much more precarious as a result of the correspondingly greater tensions that existed within them. This was particularly so in the case of households whose heads were also heads of major or maximal lineages. There were tensions between the head and his potential heir or heirs; there were rivalries among these heirs and between them and the more successful of their father's slaves and servants; and there were suppressed feuds between the women-folk, particularly those most closely related to the head by blood or marriage—feuds in which the parties sought to involve the head or his heirs.[1]

Where the household head was also the head of a local community as large as Duke Town, these tensions reached their greatest intensity, affecting a far larger number of people and involving many powerful and determined personalities. In addition to the tensions within the king's own household in Duke Town and the rivalries between divisions and cliques within his minimal and minor lineages, that sought to determine the policy of the maximal lineage or to control its head, there were also rivalries between the leading families (minimal

[1] Antera Duke's diary gives some excellent examples of witchcraft accusations resulting from tensions of this latter sort.

POLITICAL ORGANIZATION 151

lineages) of different maximal lineages competing for the office of king.

Finally, with the increasing migration of the population farther and farther away in the Duke Town and Creek Town hinterlands, there was a growing division of interests between the country-dwellers and the towns, where dwelt the majority of the wealthy and powerful and politically inclined members of the lineage and where most of these conflicts were born and bred. These tensions had normally to be suppressed and, in the case of political rivalries, thanks mainly to the authority of Egbo, there was no opportunity for their active and overt expression in political factions and fights.

It is not very surprising, therefore, to find Old Calabar society suffering from an intense fear of witchcraft (*ifɔt*). But accusations of witchcraft were not lightly made. They were followed by counter accusations, and accusers as well as accused might find themselves compelled to submit to the deadly esere poison ordeal (see above, p. 22).

Mortuary Sacrifices and Poison Ordeals

So long as the head of a maximal lineage remained alive, tensions and fears within his household and household group were mostly suppressed, but his death provided an opportunity for their release by aggressive action which, in the case of a king of Duke Town, became so uncontrolled that the results could only be described as catastrophic. Hope Waddell writes, in a description of Eyamba V's death: 'It diffused terror through the town. . . . The slaves fled in all directions. His brothers and nephew [who succeeded him as Archibong I], with trusty attendants, proceeded to search the houses, and immolate whom they could find. Entering a yard, they cried to their followers, "Shut the gate, and if any escape, see you to it"; and then strangled its inmates. . . . Armed men guarded the paths leading from the town, that none might escape to the farms and give the alarm; while others were despatched thither to seize or slay whom they could find, by road or river, in house or field.

152   EFIK TRADERS OF OLD CALABAR

'For the king's interment a great pit was dug, wide and deep, inside a house, and at one side of it a chamber was excavated, in which were placed two sofas. On these the body was laid, dressed in its ornaments, and a crown on its head. Then his umbrella, sword, and snuff-box bearers, and other personal attendants, were suddenly killed, and thrown in with the insignia of their offices; and living virgins also, it was said, according to old custom. Great quantities of food, and trade goods, and coppers were added; after which the pit was filled, and the ground trampled and beaten hard, that no trace of the grave might remain. . . .

'Eyamba had many wives, of the best families in the country, as also many slave concubines. . . . Of the former, thirty died the first day. How many by the poison ordeal, under imputation of witchcraft against his life, we never knew. Those who were honoured to accompany him into *Obio Ekpu*, or Ghost Land, were summoned in succession, by the message, once an honour, now a terror, "King calls you." The doomed one quickly adorned herself, drank off a mug of rum, and followed the messenger. Immediately she was in the hands of executioners, who strangled her with a silk handkerchief. . . .

'Every night the work of death went on in the river, and the screams of the victims were heard both in the ships and the mission-house. Some were sent out bound in canoes, and deliberately drowned. Others returning from distant markets, chanting their paddle song, and glad to get home, but ignorant of what had taken place, were waylaid, knocked on the head, and tumbled into the river. Corpses and trunks were seen daily floating down and up with the tide, till the crews were sickened, and had to fire into them to sink them. Armed ruffians lurked in the bush by the paths, to shoot or cut down whom they could, old or young, male or female. Of the slaughters committed in the farms only imperfect accounts were obtained, for they were carefully concealed from white people. For a time it was a reign of terror which was only abating when we returned to the country. The brethren Jameson and Edgerly did all they could to stay the carnage,

POLITICAL ORGANIZATION 153

but with little effect. . . . The hecatombs offered did not satisfy *Ofiong*, Eyamba's daughter . . . she vehemently upbraided the rulers that they had not killed people enough for her father; but was answered by Archibong and Mr. Young [Eyamba's brother] that they must stop for white people and God-men made too much palaver with them about it.'[1]

This account of Eyamba V's death and obsequies should be compared with the record of those of another king of Duke Town half a century earlier made by Antera Duke (see above, p. 46). On that occasion there was apparently no disorder at all and, unless the record is incomplete, only 65 persons were sacrificed. (Nine men and women buried with him, fifty beheaded on a single occasion in the obituary ceremony, one beheaded in the ritual which gave Creek Town notice of this ceremony, and five killed in honour of the dead king by various other communities.) Only one person, Coffee Duke was accused of witchcraft and Antera's account breaks off with his refusing to submit, with his accuser, the dead king's sister, to the esere ordeal.

The custom of strangling some of his wives and slaughtering his slaves at the funeral of a great man was common throughout the Oil Rivers, the bigger the man the greater the number of both. In view of the great increase of wealth at the beginning of this period, the tendency for conspicuous waste may have been partly responsible for the ever increasing number of victims, but it does not explain the manner of their execution and the lust for killing that activated the relatives of the kings of Old Calabar in the early part of the century. Slaves and wives were not the only persons to die on these occasions. Free-born men and women accused of witchcraft underwent the esere ordeal in remarkably large numbers. Ekpenyong Eyamba (Mr. Young), in a journal shown to Hope Waddell, had recorded fifty persons who had died by esere ordeal on Duke Ephraim's death in 1847, and at Archibong I's in 1852 they were never counted. The increased number of deaths by the esere ordeal on the last occasion may have had some

[1] op. cit., pp. 336-7.

154 EFIK TRADERS OF OLD CALABAR

relation to the absence of human sacrifices, but it also illustrates the ever-increasing use of the ordeal as a political weapon. Ordinary folk might believe in the genuineness of these witchcraft accusations; the more knowledgeable recognized them as a deliberate method of removing dangerous rivals, weakening powerful houses, and settling old scores. 'Old *Duke Ephraim* . . . had begun to weaken his own family by having some of them put to death [by esere] who might covet his property, as well as rivals who might rejoice in his decease. After his death the work of destruction was continued by the late *Eyamba*, to remove opponents of his elevation out of his way, and the Ephraim family were the chief sufferers. Young Eyo told me that, one way and another, above two hundred free people died for Duke Ephraim, besides slaves without number.'[1]

Intervention of the Blood Men

Egbo was powerless to intervene on these occasions to prevent the confusion and terror into which the community was plunged on the death of a king or community head. The massacre of slaves was no concern of Egbo, while their sacrifice at funerals and the administration of the esere ordeal were 'ancient customs' which it was the duty of the society to preserve. After the excesses following Eyamba V's funeral, pressure from Europeans, working on the more enlightened public opinion, particularly in Creek Town, eventually prevailed upon Egbo to pass a law prohibiting these human sacrifices; but it lacked the force effectively to prohibit practices which most of its superior members believed in. Nor was it possible for outside agencies to do this except in very special cases.[2]

But where Egbo failed the Blood Men succeeded, at least in respect of the human sacrifices. Esere ordeals did not affect them in the same way, as the accusations were only made by,

[1] H. M. Waddell, op. cit., p. 497.

[2] As in the case of the destruction of Old Town by British Naval power in 1855 (H. M. Waddell, pp. 553-4).

POLITICAL ORGANIZATION 155

and against the town-dwelling relatives and rivals of the deceased king. They showed their power in Duke Town when Archibong I died in 1852 and they came to town in earnest. Few, if any, slaves were sacrificed and not many wives were strangled on this occasion; the Blood Men arrived too soon for that. They stood by in their thousands witnessing the death by esere ordeal of one after another of the Duke and Eyamba parties, as the leaders of these two factions accused each other's supporters of witchcraft, ceasing only when they themselves had been accused and had avoided taking the ordeal. Hope Waddell describes it thus: 'His [Archibong's] mother, *Obúma* by name, sometimes called Mrs. Archibong, from her prominence and influence, became still more distinguished at that time, and seemed to reign as queen of the town. Attributing his death, as usual, to witchcraft, she began to make his wives and others "chop nut"; and it was said also that she had broken the new law by the death of many slaves. Mr. Young [of Eyamba lineage], though taking part with her in administering the fatal test, most solemnly assured the missionaries that no one had in any way been put to death for the deceased King. The town was soon filled with bands of armed men from the plantations, who came to avenge the death of their "father". *Obúma* had called them in, having her eye on higher game than the poor wives whom Mr. Young had helped her to destroy. She directed their attention to himself, his ruthless brother, Antéro, their fierce and bloody-minded niece, Ofiong, and other members of the late Eyamba's family. . . . Several thousand armed negroes assembled in the market-place, with the chiefs and their attendants, to oblige accused parties to stand their trial [by ordeal]. . . . Mr. Young gradually drew off from the work of death; but Ephraim Duke furiously urged it on. At length a woman of some rank being accused, exercised her right of challenging an opponent, and called on Mr. Young to "chop nut" with her. It was late in the day, and he managed to get the business deferred till next morning; but took care during the night to escape on board ship, and thence, on Eyo's promise of protection, to Creek

156   EFIK TRADERS OF OLD CALABAR

Town. Thither he was speedily followed by *Antéro*, while some of the females of that family got refuge in the mission-house, which by turns sheltered both masters and slaves. . . .

'When Young's name was called next morning some one made answer for him that he would "chop" with *Obúma*, and none other. But that lady was as little disposed to be put on her trial as he; and she threatened to blow up the town if any one dared to speak to her on the subject. Nor did she merely threaten; but forthwith prepared to execute her threat, by knocking in the heads of six casks of gunpowder that were in her house, and laying a train. Known to be a woman of determination, her fell purpose created a general consternation, both in the town and among the shipping.

'When Duke Town had been for several days in that state of anarchy, the brethren wrote to King Eyo to interpose and save it' (pp. 496-8). Order was eventually restored by the personal intervention, under European pressure, of the king of Creek Town, and the Blood Men returned to their farms after all parties had 'sworn *mbiam* that no more persons should die, in any way, for the late king'.[1]

With this final orgy of esere killings, political tension seems to have eased in Duke Town. The Blood Men did not come to town when the elderly Ephraim Duke died and his funeral passed without incident. Their last appearance in Duke Town was in 1871 when Archibong II fell sick and attempts were made to discover who was bewitching him. The supercargoes on this occasion forced Archibong II to persuade the Blood Men to return to their farms under the threat of a trade boycott, and when he himself died the following year no untoward incidents occurred.

In Creek Town, political tension was never so severe. Succession to the kingship was vested in the Eyo lineage and King Eyo II and his minimal lineage were more united and more strongly influenced by European 'progressive' ideas and

---

[1] H. M. Waddell, p. 499. This is the first recorded mention of this oath which is still respected in the Ibibio and Anang country (see above, p. 20, and note 49, p. 72).

POLITICAL ORGANIZATION 157

by the Scottish Mission. Nevertheless, and despite the fact that his heir, Eyo III, was a Christian, Blood Men appeared on Eyo II's death and were only persuaded to return after the non-Christian leaders of the community had sworn *mbiam* that no human sacrifices would take place. On Eyo III's death in 1861, a few years later, they again appeared and exacted vengeance, firstly on one of his father's brothers, Egbo Eyo, who was said to have been an Egbo executioner, and whom they hanged with two of his slaves for alleged sorcery (*ibɔk*) practised against the late king; and secondly on the king's sister Inyang, who was accused by her elder sister Ansa of witchcraft (*ifɔt*) and made to submit to the esere ordeal. This was the last notable appearance of the Blood Men in town. They had established their power and their rights in the face of arbitrary action by the 'town gentry' against them.[1] In 1863 Archibong II decided a case between Eyo IV and the Creek Town Blood Men in the latter's favour.[2]

But although the Blood Men successfully challenged the power of Egbo they did not in any way supersede it. They remained an association of countrymen who could be mobilized only in emergencies, and their leaders made no attempt to play any part in town politics. Egbo continued as a centralizing legislative, political, and executive body, but with gradually diminishing authority, as effective political power passed more and more to the European elements, in particular the Consul. The process was completed when, by the treaty of 1884, the British Protectorate was established.

[1] In 1857 they appeared in Duke Town and successfully demanded the surrender to them for execution of Young Antica Cobham, who had previously, without Egbo interference, killed his father's most trusted slave, and later one of his own wives. (H. M. Waddell, p. 617.)

[2] Goldie, op. cit., p. 218.

ADDENDUM

I HAVE recently had the opportunity to visit Calabar and discuss their political system with its chiefs and elders. This discussion has elucidated a number of points which were not clear to me when I wrote this essay and on which contemporary records were obscure or definitely misleading. In regard to Egbo, for example, it seems that there were two distinct organizations in Old Calabar, one for Old Town (Obutong) and one for Duke and Creek Town combined. In the second Egbo society the head was called Eyamba and was always the Obong (king) of Duke Town, while the deputy head was called the Obong Ebunko and was the Obong of Creek Town. King Eyamba V, when he became Obong of Duke Town, preferred to be called by his Egbo title and the name Eyamba came to be applied thereafter by Europeans to his house. Calabar people of today maintain that he was not the fifth head of Egbo but the fifth member of his house to become Obong and Eyamba.

My recent inquiries have shown the Efik lineage system to be more complex than appeared from the accounts of nineteenth-century writers and later administrative reports. As already indicated in my essay, the Efik 'town' or 'family', which I have termed a 'maximal lineage', has a genealogical charter which links together, as branches of a single 'family' tree, all segments within this unit. Today, at least, and particularly in the Duke (Edem Ekpo) 'family', this charter pays no regard to the relative size of these segments. But there are also still wider genealogical charters which link together a number of these 'families' or maximal lineages into two large and ultimate 'descent groups' embracing all the Efik deriving from the two legendary founders of the original Creek Town: Effiom and Ema. The genealogical relationship thus ascribed to the 'families' of Old Calabar is as follows (families being shown in capitals):

ADDENDUM

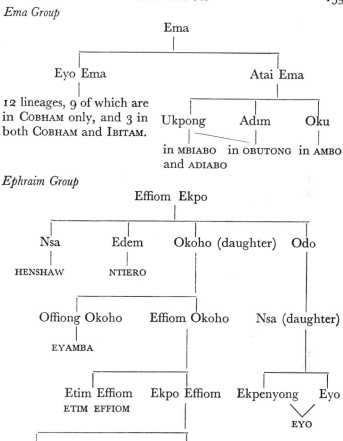

The Etim Effiom 'family', included above, does not appear to have played a very conspicuous part in Calabar politics. Hope Waddell refers to one of its Etubom as 'Adam Duke king

160   EFIK TRADERS OF OLD CALABAR

of war', but does not refer to his house, and its name is also omitted from the 1902 Native Council Rules. The Etubom ('family heads') of all 'families' in Creek Town or in Duke Town were eligible for election to the office of Obong but on account of the numerical superiority of the Okoho section of Duke 'families' in Duke Town and of the Eyo 'family' in Creek Town the office was virtually restricted to these two lines. There was a dispute between Ibitam and the rest of Creek Town over the election of Eyo II; the majority removed to Duke Town where they were given land by the great Duke Ephraim or by Eyamba V and occupied the site vacated by Henshaw when they removed to their present position. Here they took the name Akabom (*anglicé* Cobham) after one of their major lineages. The Ambo 'family' of Creek Town refer to themselves today as Mbarakom; they say that Ambo derives from a Portuguese word signifying 'loving', and was given to one of their Etubom who was very friendly towards them.[1]

G. I. JONES.

[1] But see note 42, p. 71. [ED.]

BIBLIOGRAPHY

Abridgement of the Minutes of the Evidence (taken before a Committee of the whole House, to whom it was referred to consider of the Slave-Trade), Numbers II and III, London, 1790.

ADAMS, CAPT. JOHN. *Remarks on the Country extending from Cape Palmas to the River Congo*, London, 1823.

ADAMS, RICHARD F. G. *Efik-English Vocabulary* (2nd ed., rev.), Liverpool, 1943.

BAIKIE, W. B. *Narrative of an exploring voyage up the rivers Kwor'a and Bi'nue in 1854*, London, 1856.

BARBOT, JOHN. *A Description of the Coasts of North and South Guinea* (Vol. 5 of Churchill's *Voyages*), London, 1732.

BASCOM, WILLIAM. 'Yoruba Cooking.' *Africa*, vol. XXI, 1951, pp. 125-37.

CHRISTISON, ROBERT. 'On the Properties of the Ordeal-Bean of Old Calabar, Western Africa.' *Pharmaceutical Journal*, vol. XIV, pp. 470-6, London, 1855.

COBHAM, HENRY. 'Animal Stories from Calabar.' *J. Afr. Soc.*, vol. IV, 1904, pp. 307-9.

COTTON, J. C. 'Calabar Stories.' *J. Afr. Soc.*, vol. V, 1906, pp. 191-6.

CROW, HUGH. *Memoirs of the Late Captain Hugh Crow of Liverpool*, London, 1830.

DAYRELL, ELPHINSTONE. *Folk Stories from Southern Nigeria*, London, 1910.

DONNAN, ELIZABETH. *Documents Illustrative of the History of the Slave Trade*, 4 vols., Washington, 1930-5.

FALCONBRIDGE, ALEXANDER. *An Account of the Slave Trade on the Coast of Africa*, London, 1788.

FORDE, DARYLL, and JONES, G. I. *The Ibo and Ibibio-speaking Peoples of South-eastern Nigeria*. London, 1950.

GASKIN, E. A. L. 'Twelve Proverbs and one Folk-Story from the Efik Country.' *Africa*, vol. V, 1932, pp. 68-70.

GOLDIE, HUGH. *Principles of Efik Grammar with Specimens of the Language*, Edinburgh, 1868.

—— *Efik Dictionary*, Glasgow, 1874.

—— *Calabar and its Mission*, Edinburgh, 1890.

GREENBERG, JOSEPH H. 'Studies in African Linguistic Classification: I. The Niger-Congo Family.' *Southwestern Journal of Anthropology*, vol. V, 1949, pp. 79-100.

162 EFIK TRADERS OF OLD CALABAR

GREENBERG, JOSEPH H. 'Historical Linguistics and Unwritten Languages,' pp. 265-86 in Kroeber, A. L. (ed), *Anthropology Today*, Chicago, 1953.

HOLMAN, JAMES. *Travels in Madeira, Sierra Leone*, &c., 2nd ed., London, 1840.

HUTCHINSON, THOMAS J. *Impressions of Western Africa*, London, 1858.

—— *Ten Years' Wanderings among the Ethiopians*, London, 1861.

—— *Intelligence Reports, Calabar Province*, 1930-1940 (unpublished).

JEFFREYS, M. D. W. *Old Calabar and Notes on the Ibibio Language*, Calabar, 1935.

LAIRD, MACGREGOR and OLDFIELD, R. A. N. *Narrative of an Expedition into the interior of Africa by the River Niger*, London, 1837.

LANDER, RICHARD and JOHN. *Journal of an Expedition to explore the Course and Termination of the Niger*, New York, 1832.

MARS and TOOLEY, (eds.) *The Kudeti Book of Yoruba Cookery* (7th ed.), Lagos, 1948.

McFARLAN, DONALD M. *Calabar*, London, 1946.

MURDOCK, GEORGE PETER. *Social Structure*, New York, 1949.

MYLIUS, E. N. *Intelligence Report on the Efik, Kwa and Efut clans* (unpublished).

OLDENDORPS, C. G. A. *Geschichte der Mission der Evangelischen Brüder auf den Carabischen Inseln* &c., 2 vols, Barby, 1777.

PLUMMER, G. *The Ibo Cookery Book*, Lagos, 1947.

READE, W. WINWOOD. *Savage Africa*, London, 1863.

SMITH, J. *Trade and Travels in the Gulph of Guinea*, London, 1851.

SNELGRAVE, WILLIAM. *A New Account of Some Parts of Guinea*, London, 1734.

TALBOT, P. AMAURY. *In the Shadow of the Bush*, London, 1912.

—— *The Peoples of Southern Nigeria*, 4 vols., London, 1926.

VON BRY, JOHANN THEODOR and JOHANN ISRAEL. *Sechester Theil der Orientalischen Indien. Warhafftige Historische Beschreibung des gewaltigen Goltreichen Konigreichs Guinea* &c., Frankfurt am Main, 1603.

WADDELL, HOPE MASTERTON. *Twenty-nine Years in the West Indies and Central Africa*, London, 1863.

WARD, IDA C. *The Phonetic and Tonal Structure of Efik*, Cambridge, 1933.

WESTERMANN, DIEDRICH, and BRYAN, M. A. *The Languages of West Africa*, London, 1952.

WILLIAMS, GOMER. *History of the Liverpool Privateers*, &c., London, 1897

INDEX

ADULTERY, 21
Age sets, 14-15
Agriculture, 12, 120
Andoni, 32, 72
Association, secret, 16-18. *See also* Egbo society.
Authority of Egbo society, 137, 144-5
of kings, 131-2
of lineage, 122-3

BLOOD MEN, xiii, 116, 118, 148-57
'Bob', 27-65 *passim*
explanation of, 67
Bonny, vii, xi, 116, 117, 119, 126, 132, 144, 147
Brandy, 27-65 *passim*
Brass, grade of Egbo society, 138, 143 and n. 3
in law enforcement, 139
Brass-work, 13
Burial, 18, 22, 24, 25, 33, 44, 46, 56, 152. *See also* Funeral rites.

CALABAR, DERIVATION OF NAME, 4
history of, 116-17, 118, 132
size of, 12
Cameroons, 4, 38, 43, 60
Chiefs, 16, 126
burial of, 25, 152-4
compounds of, 68
See also Kings.
Class system, 145-8

Cloth, 27, 51, 53, 124
Ekpe, 51, 76
patchwork, 13
romal, 39, 75
velvet, 16
young girls', 15, 40, 63, 68, 75
Comey (duty), 6, 33, 36, 46, 54, 56, 61, 62, 131
Compound (chief's), 68
Consul, British, 123, n. 2, 124, 125, 127 and n. 2, 130, 148
Councils, 122-3
Crafts, 12-13
Credit, 5, 123-4
Creek Town, 1, 3-4, 12, 24, 119-21, 128-9, 130, 151, 156
Currency, 5, 66
'Cry-house.' *See* Mourning.

'DASHES', 5, 27-65 *passim*, 66
Decapitation, 36, 45, 49, 50, 54, 57, 68, 76, 77, 143, 152, 153. *See also* Sacrifice, human.
Divorce, 14
Doctor (chop, drink, or make), 31, 34, 43, 46, 57, 60, 61, 62, 71. *See also* Medicine.
Dress, 9, 10, 32, 51. *See also* Cloth.
Drums, 17, 18-19, 31, 36, 58, 71-2, 141

164   EFIK TRADERS OF OLD CALABAR

Duke Town, 1, 2, 11, 68, 119, 120, 121, 127, 128, 129, 135, 139, 143, 149, 151, 156

EFIK CRAFTS, 12-13
  cults, 19-26
  derivation of name, 1
  language, 2-3, 74
  numbers of, 1
  religion, 19-26, 120
  territorial organization, 121
  traditions and history, 3-12, 117-20
  social life and organization, 12-18, 120-4, 146, 150, 158
Efut, 4, 69, 121, 123
Egbo Society, vii, xii, xiii, 16-18, 49, 27-65 *passim*, 66, 69, 71, 73, 74, 76, 77, 135-7, 158
  agents of, 140, 142, 143, n. 3
  authority of, 70, 144-5
  grades of, 16, 137-9
  'King Egbo', 28, 43, 44, 45, 54, 55, 59, 138, 139, 140
  organization of, 139-40, 158
  political function of, 140-2, 144-5
  sanctions of, 142-4
Ejagham Ekoi, xii, 1, 66, 136
Ekpe Society. *See* Egbo Society.
esere (poison ordeal), 22, 153, 154, 155, 156
European goods, 5, 8-9, 27-65 *passim*, 124

FAMILY, 122, 130, 131, 150
  polygynous, 13
'Fattening house', 15
Fishing, 12, 37, 39, 117, 120
  fishermen, 30, 40
Folklore, 18
Food, 10-11, 12, 68, 74
Funeral rites, 23-6, 46, 76, 152-4. *See also* Sacrifice, human.

GOATS, 27-65 *passim*
God basin, 31, 34, 43, 27-65 *passim*, 71
Gunpowder, 5, 27-65 *passim*, 70
Guns, 5, 10, 12, 27-65 *passim*

HOSPITALITY, EFIK, 10-11, 68
'Houses' (Efik), viii, xi, xii, xiii, 13-14, 122 and n. 1, 132-3, 158
  Ekpe (palaver house), 16-17, 75
  dwelling-houses, 8-9, 74
Hunting, 12

IBIBIO, vii, xi, 1, 3, 7, 13, 74, 77, 117, 120, 123, n. 2, 126, 133, 136
  language, 2-3, 74, 132
Ibo, 117, 133, 136
Inheritance, 14

JUDICIAL PROCEDURE, 67, 127, 143

KINGS, 125-32, 151, 158
  authority of, 131-2
  list of, 129
  selection of, 128-30

INDEX

Kwa, 2. *See also* Qua.

LANGUAGE, ANDONI, 72
  Efik, 2-3
  Ibibo, 2-3, 74
  Qua, 73
Leopard Society. *See* Egbo
  Society.
  human leopards, 136 and
    n. 2
Lineages, xi, 117, 122-3, 128,
  134-5, 147, 149, 150-51,
  156, 158
  maximal, 122-3, 128, 129,
    130, 132-5, 149, 150-51

MANATEE, 55, 77
Markets, 12-13, 152
Marriage, 14, 15
  prohibitions, 14
mbiam, 20, 72, 78, 156, 157
Medicines, 20-1, 26, 71, 72,
  76
Mission, Church of Scotland,
  ix, 3, 8, 12, 117, 125
Mourning, 22-3, 50, 56
  -house, 23, 34

NAMES, EFIK, 66, 72, 73, 75
  anglicization of, 67, 69, 70,
    72, 126
  slave, 78
Nyamkpe, grade of Egbo
  society, 138, 139, 147

OATHS, 20, 72, 149 and n. 2
Obong (*ɔbɔŋ*), 25, 31, 72,
  75, 121, 126, 130 and
  n. 3, 158

Opobo, vii, xi, 116, 117
Ordeals, 22, 27-65 *passim.*
  151-6 *passim. See also
  esere.*

PALAVER, PALAVER-HOUSE,
  27-65 *passim*, 67
Palm-oil, 6, 42, 116, 123 and
  n. 2, 124, 131
Palm-wine (*mimbo*), 11, 27-
  65 *passim*, 71
Parrot Island, 27-65 *passim*,
  69
Pawns, 35, 44, 58, 59
Pidgin english, viii, 71
'Plays', 23, 26, 45, 49, 50,
  51, 57, 73
Polygyny, 13
Population, 1, 119-20

QUA, 73, 123 and n. 2, 130,
  n. 3, 136. *See also* Kwa.

REINCARNATION, 20
Religion, 19-20, 71
Riddles, 18-19
Rods, 6, 27-65 *passim*, 66, 137

SACRIFICE, 34, 49, 57, 58
  human, 36, 45, 48, 49, 50,
    54, 57, 74, 76, 117, 118,
    139, n. 2, 141, 151-7
    passim
  See also Decapitation,
    Slaves.
Schools, viii, 8
Slave-trade, vii, 4-8, 27-65
  passim, 116-17, 142

166 EFIK TRADERS OF OLD CALABAR

Slaves, 16, 24, 25, 69, 118, 134-5 138, 145-8, 152,
numbers of, 7
status of, 146-7, 148
treatment of, 75, 77, 134-5 148
Social organization, 120-4, 146
Spirits, 20, 26, 120 and n. 2, 136-7
water, 70
Supercargoes, 6, 124-5, 127, 129, 130, 131, n. 3, 142

TRADE, 123-4
oil, vii, 123

'trust', 4-5, 67
See also Slaves.
Twins, 62, 77-8

ufɔk, 13, 122, n. 1

WARDS, 122, 126-7, 132-3
Widows, 23-4
Witchcraft, xii, xiii, 21-2, 75, 78, 150, 151
Women, position of, 145-6
Wood-carving, 13

YAMS, 10, 11, 28, 30, 36, 40, 41, 73

Printed in Great Britain by
The Camelot Press Ltd., London and Southampton